My
Lady Parts

My Lady Parts

A Life Fighting Stereotypes

Doon Mackichan

CANONGATE

First published in Great Britain, the USA and Canada in 2023
by Canongate Books Ltd,
14 High Street, Edinburgh EH1 1TE

Distributed in the USA by Publishers Group West
and in Canada by Publishers Group Canada

canongate.co.uk

1

British Library Cataloguing-in-Publication Data
A catalogue record for this book is available on
request from the British Library

ISBN 978 1 83885 636 6

Typeset in Garamond MT Std 12/15.5 pt by
Palimpsest Book Production Ltd, Falkirk, Stirlingshire

Printed and bound in Great Britain by Clays Ltd, Elcograf S.p.A

To Louis, Ella and India

'Pictures of perfection, as you know, make me sick and wicked'

Jane Austen

'Resistance is the secret of joy'

Alice Walker

'Make yourself one small republic of unconquered spirit'

Rebecca Solnit

CONTENTS

Introduction   I

The Wild Child   5
The Clown   13
The Angry Young Feminist   19
The Stupid Tart   29
The Feed   45
The Nice Mum   51
The Desperate Prostitute   63
The Rule-Breaking Rebel   69
The Trailblazer   81
The Selkie   99
The Hot Lesbian   117
The Deranged Mother   125
The Primadoona   141
The German Air Hostess   149
The Alcoholic Single Actress   157
The Desperate Cougar   169
The Ball-Breaking Dominatrix   175
The Hard-Bitten Detective   189
The Complicit PA   193

The Disruptor   201
The Sexy Older Woman   205
The Hag   217

Epilogue   227
Acknowledgements   231
Further Reading and Select Bibliography   235

INTRODUCTION

As a child I kept a diary. I kept a record of my day, what I wore, what I ate, what walks I took, almost like a hospital log, a bit sterile but with the odd silly drawing of my pet parrot spouting his latest learnt phrase. It helped me tidy the vastness of everything, to make sense of it all, and perhaps stopped me feeling lonely. I abandoned this pursuit in my late teens and twenties, too busy being in love, forging my own path, and perhaps this love stopped me writing. I took it up again in my early thirties, at the advice of an older actress I was working with, while juggling two new babies and a theatre tour. I'm glad I did – there was certainly much more that I needed to make sense of. And I kept going. This memoir is a selection of some of those stories.

I sat down at the beginning of lockdown and reread all the diaries. Then I wrote down some of the stories, not with an aim to publish – it was more like an exercise for myself – but a sudden need to sew all those books together. Some of them I felt needed to be heard, some not, so I sent a few chapters to a few agents, picked the very best one, and began the less joyous task of finding the book I wanted people to read. I had to find what was trying to come out of this ugly lump of clay – shaping, reshaping, cutting away, losing hope, abandoning it, coming back to it, and slowly with the help of my editor finding the stories that needed telling – thousands of words crossed out (I write in longhand) until I began to see something I could imagine others reading. So, three years on, it has its shape and I'm handing it over.

To avoid disappointment, here are a few things that you won't be hearing about in this book. You won't be hearing about my day in a New York recording studio, improvising with Michael Caine, what my holiday was like at Danny DeVito's house, why I chose to turn down sleeping with Andy Warhol (when he was going through his bisexual phase), which type of cigarettes John Goodman and I shared on breaks while filming *The Borrowers*, what Julie Walters wrote to me in a letter, or what Maggie Smith and I talked about backstage at Chichester Theatre. No, no, no. Sorry. None of that! I also won't be telling you what Steve Coogan and Matt

Berry are like, or if Chris Morris is a 'nice bloke', and if I found John Malkovich intimidating to work with. Sorry. No, no, no. What you will be getting is a selection of stories, front and backstage, of a life so far spanning forty years 'in the business'. From the bear pit of the stand-up comedy circuit in the early Eighties to appearing in some groundbreaking comedy shows, from *The Day Today* to *Smack the Pony* and beyond. About being a working mother in a business that does not exactly welcome babies and children; about tragic life events, survival and single motherhood. It's about putting food on the table without selling out, and continuing to create in the chaos.

My hope is that we can all see the vital need to cast off the cobwebs of compliance and fear, and to find our place – not keeping our voices down but coming out of the 'twilight of passivity' into the joy of the fight and the light.

One

The Wild Child

Casting Call

Child actor required (aged seven to nine), no experience necessary. She is a wild child, always muddy, always outdoors, and likes to eat gravel. She excels at mimicry and physical comedy. Discipline, including smacking, will not deter her. She will shun authority and loathe her incarceration in a classroom.

Growing up, I had no burning desire to become an actress. I did however passionately want to be a nurse, and hounded my younger brother, Blair, in my nurse's outfit, wrapping him from head to toe in bandages and forcing him to endure the stethoscope, the thermometer and regular lie-downs so I could play the bedside heroine. It could be said to be my earliest role. I have no idea where this passion came from (let's hope not the *Carry On Nurse* film). I keenly felt other people's pain and generally wanted them to feel better – so this naturally segued into entertainment. Laughter cured tears, lowered heart rate and vastly improved mood.

Primary school seemed like a hideous assault on my freedom. I preferred the anarchy of our garden, which, during the holidays (the only times worth living) was filled with an array of children from other countries. The lovely house we lived in, in suburban Sunningdale, just off the golf course, had a long garden, a Wendy house and magical train tracks at the very end of the garden. It also had to be paid for by regularly being filled with children whose rich parents from Milan or Düsseldorf didn't really want them for the long summer, Easter and sometimes Christmas holidays. So, they came to us, and we spent our time creating shows for the grown-ups. They became my earliest theatrical cast: extras delivering lines off and feeds, dressers and prop makers. It's highly likely that I was the lead, the director, choreographer and dramaturg, and with a large trunk of excellent clothes – my father's ex-army jackets, my mum's gaudily flowered Fifties dresses and rejected moth-eaten fur coats – we certainly put on diverse, if not entirely democratic, shows involving physical comedy, clowning, Italian, German and French accents, songs and a good smattering of tears and tragedy. Snacks were provided for parents and their guests (it was the Seventies, and there was always a drinks party), but God help them if they chatted or ate too loudly. We required utter focus and attention, laughter and, of course, applause.

We had an eclectic menagerie of animals that were also invited into the stalls to watch: a pet goat called Chanel, a Border collie, a spaniel, a ginger cat and a free-flying African grey parrot called Fred who heckled with 'Stop it, you're BAD. BAD!' in my father's voice (who hated him) and trills of laughter in my mother's voice (who adored him). Was this where the seed was sown? The joy of making people laugh or cry (or at least pretending to), the ensemble effort? The storytelling? The bossing people about?

My first primary school was a very unhappy time, although I had begged and begged to go to school early. We had a brutish headmaster, Mr Pitt, who looked like a more sinister Blakey from *On the Buses* and terrorised the school. He was tall and stick-thin, with a well-groomed moustache and a black cloak. If anyone was late for assembly, he would make them wait until nearly the end, then they would have to walk up the middle of the hall and be humiliated by speaking their excuse to the whole school. Once I went into school in slippers by mistake and had to walk to the front. I often felt physically sick if we were late, and I would catch him in secret places within the building admonishing a terrified child who had misplaced a lunch box or spilled a drink.

Breaktime was freedom. I would tear down to the school monkey bars, hook one knee over and get a crazy momentum going, creating full somersaults. It was my way of releasing the fear. One breaktime, a young boy came up to me, my age – perhaps eight or nine – and told me that some boys wanted to see me. I walked up to the top of the playground, where I was ushered into a circle of boys. I was told to lift up my skirt and pull my pants down. I did so. Why? As they sniggered and touched themselves, I felt deep, deep, burning humiliation. I was finally let go and skipped back down to the bars to show them I didn't care, but there was a feeling as though everything had changed. I never played on the bars again. I had been exposed and degraded. A little thing but also a very big thing. I felt shame.

I was unable to tell my mother for quite a long time, but she could see I wasn't myself. I felt I was 'bad', and I remember the feeling getting so big that I finally had to tell her. We went up to the school, where I had to identify the boys, and I remember I was made to feel like it was a huge waste of time, that I was being neurotic and attention-seeking. One by one they each had to apologise to me.

And then I became a pariah. The whole school knew, and I became the girl always at the edge of the playground, never invited into the girls' skipping circle, somehow tainted by this incident. So many women have experienced so very much worse than this. It just steals a little bit of the light in your soul.

This school became more and more unbearable, me crying at the gates each morning until finally my mother moved me to another one. The escapism I found in the stories and shows we performed as a rag-tag bunch of young kids in the garden set the blueprint for my later love of theatre – these children were perhaps also feeling displaced, lonely at first, then increasingly part of a community. Our garden was my first stage. I had a trusted audience who loved me: pets, family and friends, a group of displaced young ones from around the world. I could be noisy, dirty and outside most of the day. School was simply a prison. It was then that I began to write a diary and record ideas for shows and stories. It is highly likely I was the heroine: tribal warrior princess, magnanimous queen surrounded by courtiers, saviour of animals in peril – basically, kickass heroines, who are still all too rare in the stories we are telling today.

Then, aged eleven, horror of horror, my parents announced we were moving. Where? we children wailed. Across the golf course? No, to the wilds of Fife. The East Neuk of Fife, Upper Largo, and we were going soon. They sold it to us as a marvellous adventure. The house was like a palace, the sea on our doorstep, a new school and new friends. We had no idea what to expect but we tried to be brave. A month later, we were suddenly, and brutally, ripped from our soft southern comfort and garden theatre promenades, and deposited, in winter, to a Regency manse in Fife, Scotland, where we lived for the next five years.

We arrived by sleeper on 16 December 1974 in a force nine gale. The roar of the wind in the trees outside was epic as they thrashed and groaned at the entrance to our freezing new home. 'When are we going home?' my little sister asked. My parents' silence was deafening.

Whisky and electric blankets were unpacked. The next morning, I set off along the country roads to get to the sea. The landscape was so unfamiliar, so wild and lonely and beautiful; we had previously lived in the commuter belt of middle England in Surrey, on Sunningdale golf course, with its carefully controlled fairways, small stands of pine and tiny choked streams. Here was anarchy. The hedges were a riot of unknown vegetation, the likes of which I had never seen, a vast treasure chest of unfamiliar wildlife. Thistles ten foot high, majestic oaks hundreds of years old. Fields full of sheep or young bullocks. But always the sea ahead. I sped on, my hands frozen to the handlebars, simply unable to stop or turn back. I was entranced and under a spell, euphoric. This first intoxicating immersion into real nature gave me a lifelong yearning in my bones for wilderness – and the sea. A deep love of nature seared into my cells. Outside in the wilds, where I spent much of the next five years, was where I felt my truest self. The wild child in me responded to the landscape and I would spend whole days walking the forests and beaches. This was freedom, and I was triumphant.

Two

The Clown

Casting Call
Young girl aged twelve, fish out of water, hides in toilets at school and is bullied. Uses comedy and powers of mimicry to overcome her bullies and is finally accepted. Skinny, with lank hair and knobbly knees.

Darkness in Scotland was swift in winter, falling each day around 3 p.m., then sudden stars. I would travel to and from school on the bus in the starlight in those brutal early months, learning how to navigate a pitch-black road by slowly making out the silhouette of our house. My sister attended the local village primary school in Upper Largo, and my brother was dispatched to the private Dundee High (boys needed the better education as future bread-winners; girls were likely to become secretaries or homemakers so state school would do).

I found myself on the first day at Kilrymont School, on the outskirts of St Andrews, crushed by a thousand children outside the closed doors where, to my deep embarrassment, my mother had driven me in our old Jaguar in a fur coat, not looking unlike Grace Kelly. We were like zoo specimens, the object of much hilarity. It wasn't an auspicious start.

The glass doors were finally opened and we were borne along a semi-stampede into the school. I could barely understand what anyone was saying, and was given a maths test to access my academic ability (I failed, and was consequently relegated to the bottom stream). My memories of the first few weeks are of sheer panic, fear and self-consciousness. I had a piping English accent, I was tall and gangly with long greasy hair, and I was freezing. No one talked to me, so I hid in the toilets in breaktime. I even hid between the coats in the cloakrooms, as my mother had insisted that I wear a pair of 'bloomers' – a sort of thermal, purple knicker-bocker – as we weren't allowed tights (legs were pinched by some teachers to check for flesh-coloured tights). Once, one of the scary girls who taunted me in the corridors yanked me around to the side of a playground wall, and my skirt was repeatedly pulled up to the delight of a horseshoe of girls, with much hilarity and yells of 'Let's get a look at yer bloomers'. Much shoving, pushing and disgrace ensued, but I realised to my joy and a deep-seated need to survive that my powers of mimicry could swerve a good kicking, and I launched into Basil Fawlty. 'No, no, stop it! Stop it at once!' A silence fell, then explosive laughter, before an ominous instruction to 'Dae that again'. So, I then became Sybil, and, of course, the icing on the cake, Manuel. The girls loved it. I had gone from victim to entertainer in a few brave sentences.

'Who else can ye dae?' Racking my brain, I tried anything to divert and make them laugh: Stanley Baxter, Freddie Starr, Dick Emery, the Queen. It was a glorious revelation that laughter averted a good battering, and slowly as my accent changed to drop the English tones, like a worn-out chrysalis, I became accepted in my role as 'the clown', and more people were brought in to listen. I suppose it was my first stand-up comedy routine.

My English teacher at the time, Mr McKay, smoked at his lectern and brought *Macbeth* to life. He persuaded me to join the drama group – my first role being the bitchy upper-class queen in Brecht's *Caucasian Chalk Circle*, followed by a whole host of nasty villains that primarily required an English accent and a vicious skewering of the upper classes. Comedically it was win–win; I muscled into every play going as we had a thriving and inspiring drama club. I loved it, but I still didn't have a burning desire or knowledge that this was my path in life or even a career. It was fun. I made friends. I had found my tribe.

I left Scotland to attend Strode's College in Egham to do my A-levels (English, history and French – I'm not sure a drama course was even invented then). After Scotland, and the long distances, the isolation, I reconnected with old friends and went sort of wild. I could speak in an accent I was familiar with, I could wear what I wanted. I was euphoric. I rarely walked anywhere, just danced and leapt and spun, and I fell in love.

I was a flaky student. I wasted time and was full of bluster and mischief in class, always doing impressions of the teachers, walking perilously close behind them in corridors. I drew silly cartoons of imagined love affairs between members of the class and passed them around. I terrorised my French teacher, and even though I was proficient in the language, I did precisely no work. I liked my English teacher but played stupid tricks on him, for instance making the whole class go into the Portakabin next door pretending we'd got the wrong class, snickering and watching while he waited for us all. We thought it was hilarious.

The head of the English department took me aside one day and told me I should do AS-level English; the consensus was I could get into Cambridge. I just wasn't interested. I was in love with a beautiful guitarist who had a car. I tried reading Chaucer and gave up, and politely declined their encouragement. From playground clown in Scotland to class clown in England, I gave my A-levels very little attention, apart from English. I was an avid reader of plays: Arthur Miller, Tennessee Williams, Chekhov. A seed must have been sprouting because I applied to do drama at uni.

I decided Manchester University was the one for me, loving the course, the town and the tutors. But my grades weren't good enough. I had turned down other universities – I knew it had to be Manchester – so the next day I travelled up there on a train and demanded another interview. I interrupted a rehearsal trying to find a tutor whom I had liked on my first visit, and was told 'this isn't how things are done'.

I was told to wait, that no one was available, to go home, but I refused, got interviewed eventually and went back to London on the train a very happy teenager. In my interview, I gave a brave and utterly flawed description of Brecht's *Galileo*, the last play I had seen at the National Theatre. I hadn't understood a word of it. But I was very good at pretending, and I did just that.

Three

The Angry Young Feminist

Casting Call

Hot-headed, shaven-headed young 'lady' wanted, aged nineteen — goes to Greenham Common and every march going. Wears men's coats and monkey boots, is opinionated and loud, shouts about 'the patriarchy' and dumps pornographic magazines on the floors of newsagents. Intimidating, brazen.

It was 1981, and Manchester was burning. My parents and I were navigating the smouldering streets in my father's Jaguar, trying to find my halls of residence. I was eighteen. A riot had begun in Moss Side and spilled into Rusholme, where my digs were. I was sure the car would be targeted, and lay on the back seat terrified, mortified every time my father, in his cut-glass English accent, stopped to ask people for directions. 'Excuse me, my man . . .'

My mother and father were driving me from Surrey to Manchester to my new university. As we drove through the city in the mizzling grey weather – something I would have to get used to for the next three years – the streets were a sorry sight of post-riot, boarded-up shops, restaurants and pubs. Having spent my formative years in the open countryside, this was the first city I had ever lived in, and it was both shocking and thrilling. My halls of residence were a six-storey, prison-like new build, tiny bedrooms with grey breeze-block walls and single beds, and a communal kitchen. My mum trilled about, making the best of it, putting up posters of French Impressionists and getting the lighting right, while Dad stood outside, next to his XJS Jaguar, smoking and making sure it wasn't stolen or keyed – then suddenly they left.

Manchester University's Department of Drama was a mixed bunch of new students, and I remember one young man wearing a tweed jacket with a blue 'Vote Tory' rosette on it being spat at by three older women in their final year. I was aghast. But then my tight red drainpipes and stripey pyjama top were also sneered at (I was just following Johnnie Fingers from the Boomtown Rats). One of the women said, 'What are you wearing those for? Men?' I was proud of my fashion sense: a bit punky, loud, jumpers full of holes – a bit early Vivienne Westwood (although I'd never heard of her). I didn't dress to be 'sexy' or 'for men'. I felt utterly shocked by their aggression, and on my first day of my new drama course it felt very belittling. Was I meant to wear baggy trousers? Dungarees? Was there a feminist uniform that I didn't know about?

It was an unfortunate incident that triggered memories of my early years in Scottish playgrounds, but I didn't change my 'look'. I'd learned about bullies and held my ground. Later, I would attend marches with these women; I was just upset at their sense of superiority over a fledgling feminist when they should have been mentors.

Manchester did indeed introduce me, at lightning speed, zero to sixty in about six weeks, to left-wing politics and radical feminism. Our tutors extolled the Marxist theories of Brecht and actively encouraged us to stand on the steps of the students' union and throw eggs at the Tories, visit Greenham Common, or go on marches. Yes! My real schooling had begun:

politics was seamed into everything from our work to our clothes, to how we spent our free time – going on Reclaim the Night marches, supporting the CND, vegetarian cafés, benefits for the miners, refugees. It seemed everyone was getting involved. It was alive, angry. I felt a burning excitement on my first Reclaim the Night march – thousands of (mostly) women marching all night through Manchester, dressed however they wanted, but highlighting the cause in mostly skimpy outfits – the 'asking-for-it' outfits: revealing bra tops, short skirts, heels. I remember a lot of us festooning ourselves with fairy lights and chanting until we were hoarse: 'Whose streets? Our streets!' There were banners and a lot of drumming, and for the first time I understood the importance of street protest. Also, how I had always covered myself up at night. Even on my bike I would wear a big coat, always looking out for groups of men going the other way. So little has changed – it's not about street lighting or carrying mace, it's the culture, and we are still wading in the very ugly waters of misogyny.

In contrast to this, in tutorials I felt painfully shy. Everyone seemed so erudite; they discussed intellectual concepts and used words I didn't understand. I felt overwhelmed but galvanised. I wanted to have something to say in response to a piece other than 'Yes, I thought it was really powerful'.

In my first couple of weeks, I excitedly put my name down on the drama department board for up-and-coming productions that were being put on by the older students. But I didn't ever seem to get the part. I frankly had no clue how to audition, except to learn the words and look doggedly above the director's head. I began to think I had chosen the wrong course.

My first big break was to symbolise syphilis in dance form in an experimental version of Ibsen's *Ghosts*. The director asked me to reveal a breast halfway through the dance by clawing at myself; I politely declined. The first of a very long list of invitations from directors for me to get naked – 'pop your top off' was a well-used phrase in film and TV auditions. (Now, aged sixty, it's more likely to be 'pop your top back on'.) I also danced, in a yellow body stocking, the 'Banana Dance' in Kurt Weill's *Silver Lake*, to great reviews! Maybe I was a dancer? Then I focused on choreography, organising a protesting drama class into a huge Russian-inspired dance epic when we staged a Mayakovsky play. I was good at shouting and bossing people around – could this be my forte?

It wasn't long before I made the leap to trying my hand at directing – first *Woyzeck* by Büchner – but I became a kind of control-freak perfectionist, always thinking the actors weren't concentrating, always wanting to show them how to do it. I was just casting about trying to find what actually inspired me.

Our drama department staged *Women of Troy*, and I played the raving seer Cassandra, waving my arms about and incanting 'Fly Trojans, fly!' My tutor told me that a famous actor, Tim Pigott-Smith, had seen it and wanted to meet me. We had lunch in a special professors' dining room, and he told me that I had a rare and dynamic charisma! Heady words. I felt elated and decided I was an actress again.

How impossible, in your twenties, to have any idea of what you want to do. Act? Choreograph? Direct? Write? Maybe all of the aforementioned? Luckily, my course let me try everything. I'm hugely, hugely grateful that I went to Manchester University and not Cambridge. I learned so much more about life, politics, feminism, the activism of marching and protest, visiting Greenham Common, raising money for the miners. It was the canvas for the rest of my creative life.

But I was still unsure about how to express

myself or what I was actually good at. My very first stand-up comedy routine was performed to a women-only audience in the cellar bar of the students' union at Manchester University. I was aghast at 'The Women's Board' in the union and the absence of any names put down for an upcoming cabaret night. While all the surrounding boards bristled with vitality: Rowing! Rugby! Debate! 'The Women's Board' looked dysfunctional and slightly embarrassed. I put my name down and then had a three-week panic attack as to what I would perform. Studying drama at Manchester University filled my mind with wonderful roles and made me naïve as to the number of opportunities I could expect as a young female graduate in the Eighties: in reality, nothing was panning out as expected. I was auditioning for parts and not getting them, so I decided to take matters into my own hands.

I decided to write some monologues and perform them, on a dimly lit disco floor that was tacky with cheap cider. I had rehearsed the pieces in my student bedroom in Rusholme, a damp six-by-six box room with mushrooms and centipedes festooning the walls. I felt terror and excitement, which I decided must be the right combination.

My first monologue featured an actress walking onto a stage to perform a Shakespeare piece for a director deep in the shadows, and being asked by said (male) director, after every couple of lines, to remove an article of clothing.

Actress

Willow, willow, willow . . . sorry? (*Peers into darkness*) My top? Oh . . . yes, of course (*Removes her top*) What hath displeased my Lord that . . . sorry? My vest? Umm . . . yes.

I ended up stripping down to bra and pants. In the end, the director asks if I can type. It was a classic clown routine of embarrassment through reluctant compliance, but it highlighted the innate sexism I already knew was seamed into the system. I had auditioned for male directors at uni and felt wholly patronised and sexualised. One had said to a mate, 'Imagine those legs wrapped around your neck.'

The second monologue was in the form of a rap performed by a secretary who was being harassed by her boss.

I've got a job, it's 9–5, I am a secre*tary*,

I've got a boss, his name is Bill, and he's all fat and
   hairy.
Tippex, Toppex, VAT and superannuation,
Filing cabinets, ledgers, loans, cash cards, calculations
I make the coffee, make the coffee, don't forget the
   Sweetex etc. . . .

I can't remember any more, but you get the gist.
The year before university I had worked as a secretary for a group of predominantly male traders in
the City. I was eighteen and objectified, patronised,
ignored and touched up; somehow that all came out
in a rap. It lit me up from the inside. I found I could
use my experience viscerally and take some degree
of control over it.

I performed three monologues to around thirty
women in the cellar bar for the women-only cabaret
night. I was the only person who had put her name
down, so it was a solo show. I had a chair in the
centre of the dance floor and the lights were still
flashing from the disco. The women formed a circle
around me – quite a radical bunch, shaven heads,
dungarees, short leather skirts and ripped fishnets.
And they laughed. And at the end, they cheered for
ages. I was aghast; it had worked. It had physical
and character comedy, pathos and politics.

What I felt that night was a euphoric synergy of comedy and sexual politics. I was a fledgling feminist, young but already angry. I had been clattering with nerves as I stood waiting in the shadows of that disco floor but afterwards I was elated, validated, powerful. I had taken a brave step and, yes, I had been prepared to fail; instead I felt I'd found something. I wasn't sure what, but it felt good. Stand up comedy at that time was an almost exclusively male preserve but I wanted to shoulder in with a new form. There was not a great history of female 'clowns' or 'stand-ups'. I wasn't following in anyone's footsteps. I was creating something new.

Four

The Stupid Tart

Casting Call

Very attractive, versatile comedy actress, early twenties, required to play Cinderella in our 'alternative panto' for ITV. She is your typical bimbo, dimwit 'Essex girl' who loses everything as well as her slipper (her dignity and her knickers). Actress must be able to play the comedy of sexy and stupid.

Landing in Brixton post-uni, in a council estate called Angell Town, I hustled for gigs while waitressing until, finally, I was making enough to live on. I perfected my act: physical humour, sexual politics, misogynistic raps, beatboxing and fighting Ken and Barbie dolls.

If there was a march for the poll tax or to protest against the David Alton bill, I would tailor my writing and acting to it, and perform at the end of the march in whichever pub wanted it on their bill – the Old White Horse in Brixton being a favourite. They would often choose more radical and less mainstream acts for their line-ups and I was often booked. It was also my local!

(David Alton was the Liberal MP for Liverpool who introduced the Abortion Amendment bill in 1987 that aimed to reduce the time limit for women to procure an abortion from twenty-eight to eighteen weeks. 'No return to the back streets!' and 'Fuck the David Alton bill!' rang out along the streets of Whitehall, along with drums, whistles and loud-hailers. Thankfully, the bill did not pass after its third reading, which cemented my belief in the power of street protest.)

In my early days of performing and getting a foot on the comedy ladder, I would perform an 'open spot', a 'try-out' of ten minutes of my act at an established comedy venue, and if it had gone well, I would get a gig for the full twenty minutes in the following weeks. Gradually, the gigs started rolling in, normally around £40 cash in hand – not much, but enough to stop me waitressing. Some venues I kept away from, due to a kind of bear pit macho atmosphere, preferring the smaller rooms above pubs, but I rarely turned down gigs. I felt most at home on stage.

I won a few awards (*Radio Times* Best Newcomer Award, Hackney Empire New Variety of the Year Runner-Up), and was told by my contemporary male stand-ups that I wasn't a stand-up, I was definitely 'an actress' because I did 'characters'. I was loud, crude and introduced once as 'pure filth' – probably because the same words were coming from a woman's mouth. No one called out male comics; they got away with it. One even said 'cunt' twenty-five times during his act, and Ben Elton had a whole comedy routine centred around the word 'tits'.

I was spotted performing in a pub in Greenwich by a male Light Entertainment producer and offered a role in *The Hale and Pace Christmas Special* to play Cinderella. I was working in an actors' cooperative at the time, and this got me my first agent. In the eyes of the business, I was finally on my way. My first TV job, proper money and a high-powered agent.

Was this my first break? I wasn't performing stand-up so I could slip into the world of Light Entertainment, but I also wasn't going to turn down what was clearly a door-opening opportunity. From radical feminist stand-up to playing the 'stupid tart' in a populist show watched by millions. Could I make her more interesting? Create a character? Or was I just 'selling out'? It's a decision I grappled with for a few days, but I trusted my gut and the next day I accepted the job. The challenge was on.

The cast was, of course, Hale and Pace, Light Entertainment darlings, Jim Davidson, ever popular for his racist, sexist rants, and, luckily for me, a very young Harry Enfield. By the early Nineties, 'Alternative Comedy' had pushed its way through the cracks of popular entertainment in a knee-jerk reaction to the offensive stereotypes peppering this pretty much all-male bunch. Comedies like the *Carry On* films, Benny Hill, *'Allo 'Allo!* and *Hi-de-Hi!* were the norm: the TV bosses knew alternative comedy was getting more popular, so they had to move with the times, tread a bit carefully to allow this transition to happen seamlessly.

I was to play Cinderella as a stupid Essex girl in a very short hessian frock – clueless, vacant but a bit sexy. My nickname at the time was Millie Tant (my friends and family called me this), after the character in the *Viz* comics. It was during this time that I was learning more about my feminism and forming strong opinions about the world. I was an active member of WAVAW (Women Against Violence Against Women). We graffitied huge sexist posters at night, shimmying up precarious ladders in Vauxhall, and continually wrote letters of complaint to the ASA (Advertising Standards Authority). I attended Reclaim the Night marches, just as I had in my university days, and my stand-up act was becoming more and more political.

This world of Light Entertainment was new to me: bright, shiny and grim. Perma-tanned males wearing pastel colours grinned out from photos along the long corridors of London Weekend Television – Brucie, Tarby, Paul Daniels, Bob Monkhouse – and, suddenly, there I was in my own dressing room: true luxury, after the fetid backstage areas of pubs or the Comedy Store where men would piss in the sink with me still there. I even had my own fruit bowl.

During the dress rehearsal for Cinderella, my leg hairs were noticed and I was hastily ushered into make-up.

Make-Up Lady
We need to shave your legs. Let's do it now during the tea break.

My Lady Parts

Millie Tant
Sorry, no, I don't want to.

(*Horrified looks*)

Make-Up Lady
Well, I'm afraid the director and the whole
team have requested it.

Millie Tant
Well . . . I feel . . . I just don't want to.

I wish I could remember more of that conversation. I know it went on for some time in a circular loop. I know I was shamed for my disgusting hairy legs. As a fully functioning feminist, I absolutely adored my legs and the hairs growing upon them. To shave or otherwise remove my leg hair was completely my own choice. But, to my credit, I held firm. I was released like a wild animal back onto the stage after refusing to comply. It is something I have taken great pleasure in doing ever since, but I felt shamed and self-conscious as I walked with as much dignity as I could muster in my little hessian dress up to the big shiny stage. The all-male camera crew (who I'd noticed passing around porn mags earlier) zoomed onto my legs for all to see, and suddenly there they were, beamed onto several huge screens above the empty, raked audience seating. My face burned crimson red, but I smiled and carried on. Having hairy legs wasn't a major radical feminist statement. It was natural, and I liked them, and luckily so did the men I chose to sleep with. The crew then started chanting lines from a well-known razor advert: 'Gillette! The best a man can get!'

There were great howls of laughter from the crew, and as you can imagine, Jim Davidson found that hilarious. I did the gig that evening, and my dear mama came along to support me. She was proud, I think: her militant stand-up daughter finally going mainstream and getting paid well, and on TV, and all her friends could watch and, well . . . I was on the right road, no? She came backstage and drank prosecco in my dressing room and was beaming from ear to ear. For my mum's sake, I was happy that she got to see her rebel daughter in a show she finally found palatable and could boast about excitedly. To her I had gone 'mainstream', surely a step up from the angry stand-up world to something altogether more acceptable: she had loved the show and could tell her friends to watch it.

As we left the dressing room Jim Davidson pointed at me and shouted down the corridor, 'Jesus! Not only has she got hairy legs, she's wearing men's shoes!' (I was wearing Doc Martens, clearly well ahead of my time.)

My mother was appalled and confused as to why I was being heckled backstage. Luckily, a very young Harry Enfield, who was playing Buttons, rescued us and took us to the bar. 'Welcome to the world of Light Entertainment!' he quipped. He offered me a role in his up-and-coming series – much less light ent – and this was the first of a raft of alternative comedy shows, but unsurprisingly these pioneering shows were almost exclusively led by men: Harry Enfield, Paul Whitehouse, *The Mary Whitehouse Experience* (a five-man sketch show), Armstrong and Miller, Sean Hughes, Nick Revell and, of course, Frank Skinner and his five failed pilots, to name a few. Sadly, even though contemporary female comics pitched their shows, they rarely, if ever, got the pilots. In the men's shows, even though the female parts were perhaps less 'stereotyped' and more 'progressive', we were essentially the straight women to the funny man.

The disrespect and aggression of that early incident just fired me up. I would give Light Entertainment a very wide berth, and focus once again on stand-up.

The stand-up circuit in the mid Eighties, as a woman, was something of a bear pit. I remember getting booed off at the Tunnel Club, a venue notorious for acts getting bottles thrown at them if they displeased the baying crowd. Jeers hurt, although maybe not as much as bottles, but if you were the only woman on the bill and you failed, you felt you were confirming the age-old adage that 'women just aren't funny'. 'Get your tits out' was a regular heckle, or very often 'quite funny for a bird' after the gig. Like being the sole female on a panel show, performing among men sets you at a disadvantage. Even with just one other woman, you feel a strength in numbers, the ability to banter on your own terms. The circuit was a solitary place. Good gigs felt tremendous, of course: elation on the bus home, mind scrolling in detail through the parts that had worked or failed. But a bad gig was like a defamation of character. You couldn't hide behind a script, a character, a camera. It was you, bare-faced, daring to perform. I always had the feeling that I sort of put my armour on before a gig. Was it really me up there performing? A heightened, toughened version perhaps, a less vulnerable version of myself. Brittle and mouthy, deemed 'filthy' because I swore and talked about sex and used my body with abandon, clowning and physicality as important as the words. But it was a boys' club, backstage all men in the dressing room, the banter, me being ignored. Rarely was I congratulated if the gig went well, and there were lonely bus rides home, feeling isolated and needing a team effort.

One of my last ever stand-up gigs was Reading Rock Festival. It was an enormous tent with a banging sound system. I arrived around 2 p.m., to be told, with long faces, that the male comics had struggled to perform, that it was a losing battle. A group of twelve Hell's Angels was ruining every act with aggressive heckling. They were pissed and they thought they were hilarious. What heckler doesn't? I was due to go on after the interval at around 6 p.m. and I had watched two acts actually abandon the stage. No one ejected the Hell's Angels. It was a rock festival. Suck it up, comics!

The interval came, and the Hell's Angels all trooped out. I was practically on my knees with gratitude. It was a huge stage, and my heart pounded as I sank a much-needed pint before the storm. The lights went down, on went the compère and back trooped the twelve Hellish Angels, armed with six-packs and bottles of Jack Daniel's. No one dared tell them to fuck off or shut up. I was introduced.

I was, as they say in Ancient Greece, 'pumped'. I was a Christian before the lions but, by God, I would go down in style. I felt angry that a small number of pissed blokes were ruining a gig for about three hundred people, and, suddenly, something replaced my nerves. Balls of steel? I took a deep breath and swaggered out.

My act began with a loud and rather proficient beatboxing routine which led to a vehement misogynist rap. The sound system was so incredible I actually sounded like a proficient rapper and, to my amazement, it shut the fuckers up!

> My name's Big Bee
> And I'm the baddest around.
> Mr Tough, Mr Sexy
> Got my feet on the ground.
> I'm also so cool,
> And I ain't no fool,
> And I've got myself
> One mighty big tool.
> My friends know me
> By the name of Thumper.
> You get yourself a girl,
> You pump her and dump her . . .

You get the gist. I gave that rap every ounce of my energy, anger and fear. It worked. The crowd roared, including the Hell's Angels. They looked stunned! *A bird! Jesus!* I didn't leave a nano-second for any interjections. I was flying. I was on a roll. The audience was with me, so happy to be watching an undisturbed act. Sexual politics, orange-peel teeth and an exploration of what lust does to a woman, clowning, many accents and impressions. I ruled that stage, and, as the act came to a close the strong winds outside were straining the guy ropes of the tent, meaning huge corners were flapping like sails in a storm, adding to the charged electric atmosphere. I reached my final punchline and a whole section of the tent lifted and flew free to the roars of the audience.

'Thank you, Reading! Good night!'

I'd blown the tent away. Literally. I realised it would never get any better than that, and I didn't want to do it any more and I wanted to take my armour off. It's not that every gig required this amount of chutzpah or balls of steel, it's that I began to feel that it was only one part of performing. A rather aggressive 'fuck you' part. Yes, funny, inventive and often hilarious, but limiting. I longed to have more subtlety, more range and more vulnerability

– in short, acting! I felt worn down by it and needed to spread my wings.

I'd grown tired of the macho culture of stand-up, the boys' club banter and competitiveness, and always being the only woman on the bill, so I decided to take a theatre job to have a break, while also subsidising myself in the bright, well-paid world of television and the safety of someone else's script. My career at the time constantly veered between the two. My first theatre role was Helena in *A Midsummer Night's Dream* at Birmingham Rep. As I waited in the canteen queue on my first day of rehearsals, someone slowly but firmly stroked my backside and murmured, 'Hmm, nice arse.'

It was a major TV star fresh from his role in my favourite soap – the nirvana of television for me (not one episode missed between the ages of eleven to sixteen). This actor was my on-screen hero. I was so shocked I sat down and said nothing.

The next day he was walking towards me down a very long corridor. My instinct was to run, but I held my nerve, and as he got level with me I grabbed his crotch and said, 'Mmm, nice bollocks.'

He never spoke to me again.

The Essex Girl, the Bimbo, the Dimwit, the Tart with a Heart, one sandwich short of a full picnic:

these descriptions pepper the roles on offer for younger women. Take this example from a recent casting call.

Camilla (personality BIMBO): Attractive and beautiful, Camilla is the office 'hottie'. She's got the job purely for her pair of legs, she hasn't got a clue what she's doing but she's good at pretending that she does.

Stories from the front line from young actresses auditioning for the part of 'The Maid' or 'The Office Hottie' include one being asked to fellate a Coke bottle, lick a pencil like it was a delicious ice cream, or else being instructed to behave like Marilyn Monroe: 'You know, pout, flutter your eyelashes, the thing you do so well'. One actress I spoke to went to the toilet during her audition and overheard the casting directors describing her.

'Yeah, he likes the one with the big tits and bow in her hair.'

Being told you had to pad your bra for the part or bleach your own hair. That being a brunette was a deal-breaker. One actress who didn't get such a part was given feedback from the famous director that she was 'sexy'. As though that should be a consolation! The stories are endless. And, sadly, still happening.

Lazy sexism, casual misogyny, things said, acts done to take you down a peg or two. From my first TV experience to my first Shakespeare in a rep theatre, the undercurrent of misogyny was impossible to ignore and hard to overcome. These microaggressions are body blows for women, yet we must keep getting up every time.

Five

The Feed

Casting Call

Versatile comedy actress wanted, mid-twenties, to play a variety of characters in this male-led pilot: sexy nurse, strict teacher, nagging wife (to name but three). Must be good at accents, open-minded and pliable, grateful and accommodating when her lines are cut. She is essentially the straight woman to the funny man.

While contemporary male stand-ups or sketch groups progressed to make radio shows, which then secured TV pilots, women just didn't have the same trajectory. We would pitch shows but, because of French and Saunders, we would be told that channels 'already had their women's show'. So many of my male contemporaries from the circuit got their own shows, yet the equally talented girls? Well, we were reduced to the magicians' assistants, the eye-candy, the feeds.

I played a long-suffering daughter in Harry Enfield's TV show; I played various characters in the Nick Revell show – a sexy nurse, strict teacher, dim receptionist, nag, trainee and superbitch. It really gave me an opportunity to showcase my versatility and range.

I didn't understand what a 'feed' was until I performed in a TV sketch show called *Five Alive*. It was sold as an ensemble sketch show but it was solely a vehicle to launch the careers of its two male stars, Brian Conley and Peter Piper. I was told by Mr Piper during rehearsals on the first day that I was 'a good feed'. Had I been sold a dud? I soon realised few of the funny lines were mine – that indeed I was there, hair curled, make-up on, brightly coloured mini-dress and heels, to 'feed'.

On some level it was pitched to me, by agents and casting directors, that performing in these men's shows was great for my CV, that it was maximum exposure, that it would increase the chances of my own show, but for women at that time – and now

– the margin of opportunity is so very slight, so small. We have many more brilliant women now fronting their own shows, rather than that male-dominated clusterfuck. But the ratio is still far from equal.

After years of upsetting my parents with my ranting politics and shaved head, doing this sketch show was sheer joy for them. I was in a prime-time mainstream comedy. I had arrived. Yet inside I felt trapped and miserable, forced to endure endless ghastly photo shoots with the two stars in the middle. Although promised my own comedy characters, these were painfully marginal: a newsreader, a trainee. It was clear I was there to support the two male leads. After this imprisoning experience, I ran screaming back to the comedy circuit. Here I would get disillusioned and lonely, so would take another TV job. That job would be another male contemporary's pilot that would then become a series, and the cycle continued. At the time, I was pitching my own shows and radio ideas to commissioners, but they were just not being picked up. I was forced – in order to make a living – to appear in these shows.

Mel Smith and Griff Rhys Jones were in the more famous echelons of alternative comedy I played various 'feeds' in. Armando Iannucci, the prominent producer and director, caught my act in a pub in

Lewisham and got me involved in a radio show called *The Mary Whitehouse Experience*. It was my first live radio show at the Paris Studios in Regent Street, alongside Dave Baddiel, Rob Newman and Punt and Dennis. I remember walking into the studio, terribly excited about the whole experience, to find they were all lying about on the floor. Not one of them said hello or welcomed me. There was a general sense of entitlement in the air, although 'entitlement' is perhaps an understatement. I was the only woman and I felt distinctly inferior. Again, 'feed' is the exact word to describe my input. One sketch required me to be a sort of Sue Pollard character. I didn't really watch TV so I had never seen her and ended up doing a sort of cod northern accent.

'That's the worst Sue Pollard impression I've ever heard,' said Mr Baddiel, who seemed to be disgusted. (It was as though I could hear his thoughts: who *is* this actress? Is it too late to get someone else?) I remember taking myself off to Green Park in the break, where I sat with a sandwich, crying, the wind well and truly taken out of my sails. It was my first ever radio recording at the beginning of my career, and it was ruined by a Cambridge-educated, entitled man-child.

The night, however, was a success. A TV series

ensued, and I was asked, once again, to be the men's 'feed'. They had a new, dynamic, charming director, who professed how very upset they were that they had offended me (via my agent) and that they were going to write me some cracking comedy in the new series. This was going to be very different. It was *The Mary Whitehouse Experience*, the television comedy that was breaking into the mainstream, and I was fortunate to be involved. The parts written for me were better. There was a modicum more respect. But cut to the live recording, and after rehearsals the director realised we were running over. The solution? All my decent comedy was cut. I was once again reduced to a minimal 'feed': whining teacher, sexy mum, nerdy scholar. I wish I'd walked. But instead I gritted my teeth and got through the show, willing it to be over. I thought I would wait for the curtain call and then politely leave. I realised, as they all piled backstage after the show, that I hadn't been invited on at the end. I was invisible. I was the 'feed'. They came off in a rage because it hadn't gone down better. They called their audience 'fucking thick' for not understanding their jokes. They railed at the stupidity of the crowd. They didn't give me a second glance and I left.

I wrote a letter to the *Guardian*'s Woman's page

outlining my experience, telling them that *The Mary Whitehouse Experience* had been a very unpleasant experience for me and that I hoped they didn't put another woman through it. Of course, they were recommissioned, but they cut 'the woman' from the rest of their shows, and I took another blow to my confidence which made me just a little more angry.

Some years later, after recording *I'm Alan Partridge* in the same iconic Paris Studios, Patrick Marber mentioned that he was writing a play and would I help workshop it at the National Theatre? It was called *Dealer's Choice*. The female role was in no way equal to the male roles in terms of emotion or story arc. Despite some little forays of improvisation in the workshop, the role remained painfully sketchy. I told Patrick to cut it. To his credit he did. In one of the reviews it said, 'It is a play defined by the absence of women.'

Hmm, I thought. The same could describe the history of comedy.

Six

The Nice Mum

Casting Call

`Apple-pie mum, early thirties, mostly`
`in the kitchen doing cooking, washing,`
`or gently admonishing our hero lead, aged`
`nine, about his school work or his messy`
`room. Sweet, pliable and the bedrock`
`of the family, she is long-suffering and`
`loving to her 'eccentric' forgetful`
`husband — two scenes at the beginning`
`and end of the film: strong presence,`
`despite her lack of lines.`

Max Stafford-Clark ran the Royal Court Theatre for fourteen years. I had auditioned for him a couple of times and not got the job. Once, the audition was in a bedroom in the Sloane Hotel, with him lying on the bed. His casting director sat next to the bed on a chair, and although she didn't leave the room, there was a whiff of Weinstein about the whole set-up. It felt tawdry, uncomfortable and patronising. I felt like a prostitute who had turned up at the hotel and now had to prove she was good. Cutting-edge new writing, one of London's most famous theatres, and its then-lauded director is lying on a hotel bed, watching a young actress blushingly work her way through her lines. I remember fixing my eyes on a plug on the bedside table thinking, This sucks.

The third time I auditioned for him, it was in a rehearsal room. The role was Princess Diana in Sue Townsend's *The Queen and I*, adapted by her from the novel, where the royal family is deposed and forced to live on a Leicestershire council estate while the republicans take over.

The brief was to turn up dressed as Di. The grimness of seeing three actresses in the waiting area with bad blonde wigs, pale-blue frocks and white tights cannot be underestimated. There was no dialogue to read at that stage; instead, we were invited to bring something of our own to read as Diana. The small yet powerful flame of indignation from the hotel bedroom audition was burning inside me as I turned up in my own clothes with my own long brown hair and proceeded to recount to Max, as Princess Diana, the sex I had tried to have with Charles the previous night. It was utterly filthy and to my total joy made the director blush deeply. Back of the net!

I had meticulously researched Diana's voice, going to the National Sound Archive and charting her voice from innocent nursery teacher – high, piping, painfully shy – to the broken, angry Di of later years, her mental health problems, her incarceration at the palace. That later voice was loaded with sarcasm, repressed tears and unspoken vitriol – the veneer of royalty cracking. I had the voice to a tee as I slid in and out of an account of the previous night with Charles.

Diana

I had slipped on a snap-fastening teddy with a peek-a-boo bra, sprayed myself with Agent Provocateur scent, a heady mix of hairspray and underwear, and I asked Charles what he'd like to do . . . He stared off into the middle distance . . . It was desperate.

It got raunchier as the director went redder. I got the job. But there was just one more thing before it was in the bag. 'Could you come over to my house tonight wearing a blonde wig, like Di?' The final humiliation. But I did it. Borrowed a wig, turned up and then stayed for dinner with his wife, but not before I'd had to read 'a bit more' in a sitting room upstairs with a bedroom door open. Power. I hadn't told him I was three months pregnant.

As you will see with my next experience, women who were pregnant were often fired or mysteriously 'let go'. This director – to his credit – accepted the fact that I could hide the bump, and I was allowed to perform. I did the job until I was seven months pregnant, my red Versace suit being let out every two weeks. The play then transferred to the West End without me. How many actresses get to work until they're seven months pregnant? Some have to take on their employers if they have the time, energy or money, but mostly they are sacked and say nothing.

Once he knew I was pregnant, said director minded his manners and the job was a delight. A memorable night was a bomb scare where we, as the royal family, plus audience, were herded into a taped-off Sloane Square, but stayed in character in case we went back in to finish the play. The public talked to us as if we were royals. The whole thing was surreal and hilariously bizarre.

After this, I was offered a sitcom with Maureen Lipman when my firstborn, India, was three months old. I had intended to stay home for at least six months, but we desperately needed the money. My partner was an actor and our finances were precarious. I demanded that the baby came with me to rehearsals and live recordings at the BBC and that we should stop for breastfeeding when needed. A friend came along too, employed as a nanny. (I hadn't negotiated extra money for childcare, but from that point on I did.) We turned up at the gloomy North Acton studios laden with the baby, changing mat and toys. Despite my agent's conversations with the BBC production team informing them that I would be bringing a nanny and a baby to rehearsals, I was met by a harassed young girl who had no idea what to do. I needed a room, obviously, to breastfeed in and for my nanny to look after and change the baby. Totally blank looks – she showed me to a green room that was full of actors smoking.

'Well, obviously, we can't be in here. Everyone's smoking.'

After much rolling of eyes, a hungry baby crying, phone calls from an irate director, it was: 'Sorry, we can't start. Doon needs a room.'

It somehow felt shameful to turn up with a baby,

but I was a mother and everything had changed. I had a sort of animal confidence but also a strong sense that I would have to fight if I wanted to work. I felt the inequality keenly. I refused to be shamed. This set the blueprint for the next two decades of my working life. I made my babies visible. They came with me. I demanded extra money for childcare if the companies wanted me so much. I often didn't get it. It was embarrassing, an encumbrance, oh God, here comes Doon: nanny, baby, mobile, changing mat, a bag of toys and a mouthful of militancy. It would have been much easier if I'd had a dog. We do prefer dogs to children in this country. I leaked milk into my costumes, and halted rehearsals and filming in order to breastfeed. I performed on *Top of the Pops* in the Glam Metal Detectives playing lead guitar in a slashed velvet catsuit literally soaked with breastmilk when India was a month old.

When she was six months old I was pregnant again. I felt far from ready. In fact, I felt shattered. But elated. I had come to realise how difficult it was to work while breastfeeding. The exhaustion and lack of sleep and having to turn on the comedy and turn off the milk. The unwelcome atmosphere on set. It was chaotic, and I knew I wanted not to have that pressure with my second born, so sacrifices were made. I was offered a role in *Fever Pitch* to star alongside Colin Firth. I would be filming on football terraces and my new second baby would be a month old – I said no. Then a big Hollywood film, *The Borrowers*, was offered – starring John Goodman, Hugh Laurie, Jim Broadbent. It was a wonderful script. I would be cast as 'nice mum', the mother to the main little boy and only top and tailing the film, a maximum of three weeks, not three months like *Fever Pitch*. It would be my first film, my baby would be three months old, and they promised a room for the baby, money for the nanny, time off to breastfeed and so on. This felt so progressive! So accommodating, when it should just be normalised. Women who have children can also still work! I did it: I brought my previous two tiny ones to a boiling dressing room in Elstree Studios. I spent long, long hours there, waiting, for lighting, sound and special effects. The nanny did her best, but nine to ten hours in a tiny room did not work. I frantically expressed milk at every feed with a huge milking machine, so that little Louis would get my milk when I was filming, and stacked the freezer up with little bags. But it was hellish. The three weeks promised as the duration of my part in the film turned into six, then it was 'rain cover', which meant sitting in the studios while the baby was at home. (If they are filming exterior shots and it rains, they have you on 'stand-by', in case they have to come indoors and shoot a scene you are in.) It is standard, but it had not been flagged up earlier and I missed weeks with my new baby. I missed the day feeds, I missed the evening feeds, I missed him. I would get home aching, both my breasts and my heart. I was missing the early ambrosial weeks, where they change every day, and learn new sounds and skills. A tiny baby and a fourteen-month-old ferried to and from Elstree with a deranged mother bursting with milk.

In the first couple of weeks on set, when I felt the tingle and needed to feed, the whole crew had to wait. It was somehow humiliating walking off, a pain in the arse, shouldn't be allowed, why haven't we sorted this? Why are babies meant to be at home or stuck in nurseries? Why can't our children be near us as working mothers? Where are the creches? My career was bounding ahead, but I felt torn. Time at home was precious, but was it really one or the other? I have heard so many stories from actresses that their careers took a serious knock when they had their babies. Some even made this a reason not to have children as it could ruin their careers. Very few actresses bring their babies to set. It is seen as an inconvenience, an intrusion, a time-wasting idea, and if you want to work and still see, and even feed, your baby, you're at a distinct disadvantage in our business. There are no creches and there is no money for childcare unless you insist that this is a contractual deal breaker. So, either actresses leave their tiny babies at home with nannies, and partners, and don't see them (a big TICK from producers), or they bring their babies and nanny with them and upset the apple cart with the extra costs and distraction (a big CROSS from producers). Or you could just stay at home and be a 'nice mum' and not do the job.

I was able to perform pregnant (twice) and bring my baby to set and have breaks for breastfeeding but only by demanding this upfront. So many actresses don't do this for fear that they will be seen as 'difficult' or 'demanding'.

Yes, I was seen as a giant pain in the arse.

Oh God, CUT! Doon has to breastfeed . . . OKAY, tea break! (Eye rolling and sighing.) But I was able to see, to feed my babies and work. The alternative was not to have my tiny baby on set with me, turn the job down and stay at home. Very few actresses brought their children to set, let alone their babies. And that has to change.

'Nice mum' has to become 'fierce mum'. She

isn't cow-like, with dewy eyes, soft and pliable; she is forced to fight to be able to be a working mum. I needed to earn, I wanted to work, and I wanted my babies with me for as long as possible.

After my second child was born, an American agent was interested. In me and in Hugh Laurie from our agency. We met her. Was I willing to spend six months of every year in the US for possibly a six-year contract? Bring babies with me, and my husband – uproot family life? Ferrying kids from America to Britain, every six months? Hugh was, I wasn't. I opted to stay local, not wanting to disrupt our new family and our domestic life, schools, friends and so on. He became a superstar. Hey-ho . . . Are women more likely to stay and fight for family or ruthlessly follow their career path? Answers on a postcard, please.

The Borrowers experience had taught me that I painfully missed the early weeks of my children's lives. Was it a sacrifice worth making? The production company had seemed accommodating, but in reality time is money and I was a giant pain. I turned down three pretty marvellous jobs after this to stay at home – not to be juggling so much, not to be achingly desperate to be in two places at once. I just chose to stay home for a while, and I'm glad I did.

But I brought my kids with me on every job after this, asked for money for childcare and made them part of the package. If you want Doon while her kids are small, they must come too.

Seven

The Desperate Prostitute

Casting Call

Ragged and broken with pockmarked skin, Evette is a prostitute in this long and dirty war — a sex worker for the soldiers, in unsanitary filthy camps, hungry and cold. She will stop at nothing to turn a trick. Hard as nails with a beautiful singing voice, desperately romantic, she thinks her first childhood sweetheart will come back for her. Deluded and increasingly an alcoholic.

When India was six months old, I got an audition at the National Theatre to play Yvette, a prostitute, in Brecht's *Mother Courage*. I had never worked at the National (apart from a two-day workshop with Patrick Marber). I got the job the same day as finding out I was pregnant for the second time. This time I didn't wait. I told them straight away. My firstborn was six months old, the job would begin in three months, and I would finish when I was eight months pregnant. That seemed a little too close.

I said I could do the job, as I had with India, into the seventh month. This time I could show the bump – what more poignant image than a pregnant prostitute scrabbling after soldiers in a long and dirty war? I spoke to the director, Jonathan Kent, who was excited by the idea and had no problem with it. Likewise, Diana Rigg, who was playing Mother Courage had no problem with it; in fact, thought it was a brilliant asset. I was thrilled. The National wasn't eight shows a week; it varied as plays were in repertory. I could do this. But the National disagreed. I was 'let go' – or shall we say 'fired'? I was aghast. Could they do that? My agent at the time had sounded disappointed when I told her of my second pregnancy. Now she refused to support me in trying to keep the job. She had two other actors at the National at this time, and when the theatre said no I asked her to go back to them and try again.

Her response was: 'Darling, best not rock the boat.'

I fired her.

I was stunned at her reaction. I was frustrated at being silenced and felt the response was deeply problematic. Then I heard that an actress in the National's current production of *A Little Night Music* had been fired a week before for being pregnant. I started calling the National now that I was representing myself. Their reason was that they didn't have a space to rehearse in the new Yvette for the final six weeks of the show after I had left. I had no agent, no job, and I was pregnant, looking after a six-month-old. And, of course, vehemently bemoaning this to anyone who would listen. I got an excellent and lucky piece of information from a friend who told me there were EU regulations protecting pregnant women: if they wanted to fire me, they would have to pay! If they didn't pay, I would sue. I called the National again with this most excellent information. The manager I spoke to was a woman. My laser-like voice detection skills led me to believe she now hated me. She tried to shame me, freeze me out and make me feel like a huge burden on her time. I was gaslit into believing that I didn't have a right to the money. Weeks of back and forth ensued. The manager wasn't always available, but I doggedly persisted. The she-wolf was howling. I said plainly that unless I was compensated, I would sue. And, while I was at it, where was the creche at the National? A shocking number of empty rooms as far as I could see, and great swathes of floor space with a small art gallery in a corner. It wouldn't have taken much to make the space work better for both actors and patrons alike. I hadn't taken any legal advice at this point. I just kept calling. But inside I was losing heart. The rehearsal period was drawing ever closer. Two weeks before the production began, miraculously, without one single letter or email, I got the job back. I performed until I was seven months pregnant. At the end of the show audience members would often exclaim, 'Oh, my God! You're really pregnant. I thought it was a cushion.'

Her pregnancy had enhanced the sadness of Yvette – her desperate situation, her loneliness and her poverty. Every time I walked out into that glorious purple amphitheatre of the Olivier carrying my unborn baby I was exultant. Victory! Now *that* was Mother Courage.

When walking out onto that stage during rehearsals, some of the younger actors (including

Martin Freeman, in his first job as non-speaking boy in cart) expressed their fear of such a giant space. Performing stand-up comedy for eight years had cauterised my stage fright. When you've died in front of two hundred squaddies at the Woolwich Tram Shed, the Olivier? Pah! Piece of piss!

After *Mother Courage* I didn't work at the National again for ten years. God! Was I that bad? The reviews thought not, but the building was furious. I continued to press for a creche.

It never happened. It still hasn't happened. Perhaps that's why so many of the technicians and crew are men.

Very little has changed in the last twenty-five years to protect pregnant women in our business. Recently, after a two-year battle (ending in a tribunal which she won), an actress, who was 'let go' from the second series of a show where her character had been established, won a paltry £11,000 that barely covered her legal costs. The reason for letting her go was that her pregnancy would 'impede the director's creative vision'. She had to be glamorous, in tight clothes, but the scene was under a minute and they could have shot it easily by covering her bump, which was not even hugely pronounced.

It was only when a fellow actor at the read-through

called her to say, 'There's a woman here who looks like you reading your part,' that she realised she had been dismissed. It simply demonstrates the double standard that women continually find themselves up against.

Eight

The Rule-Breaking Rebel

Casting Call

Actress wanted, age thirty to thirty-five.
Doesn't give a fuck: anarchic, mother of
two, in-your-face, loud and proud — to
appear in 'most offensive TV programme
ever made' and her own radio show garnering
the second highest number of complaints
ever recorded for Radio 4. Used to being
blanked in playgrounds and some social
events, she will stand up for her politics and loves a good rant.

At the end of *Mother Courage*, I was seven months pregnant with my second child. I had a small window before the birth to record a radio series, called *Doon Your Way*, which I had written and had commissioned prior to the National job. I recorded the series – eight months pregnant in a bright orange T-shirt dress emblazoned with 'Hussy' – at the BBC Radio Theatre. The show was set in a Portaloo on Peckham High Street where a pirate radio station – Flush FM – was illegally broadcasting. It starred Pam Ferris, Lesley Sharp, Phil Cornwell and Alistair McGowan among others. Jonathan James Moore was the commissioner, as it was the good old days where there was minimal overbearing editorial over-sight, and he trusted the producer, Jon Magnusson, and I don't think he had even read all the scripts. We had delightful, uncharted, uncensored anarchic freedom. I love pirate radio, I love the banter, the beats per minute, the crazy language.

'Stand clear of the bass bins! Hold tight!'

Chantal, the ubiquitous DJ, interviewed famous people played by Phil Cornwell and Alistair McGowan. It was a ludicrous, bright noisy world peppered with naff adverts.

Head O'Hair. We colour right down to the root bulb!

Athene Sex Shop – light the blue touch paper and lie well back

Characters included the Brownie, who directed us to all-night raves and chained herself to news-agent shelves to get her Brownie porn badge, and

Single Mothers' Question Time with Princess Diana. There was a Word of the Week, for example, 'Perambulate – it means to walk around a bit'. The show's themes were looking at the 'underground culture' of pirate radio – of class, race, low income, adverts made in a front room, illegal masts bristling from the tower block where I lived in Angell Town. I had spent the Eighties there, listening to all the different frequencies, but it was an unknown world to a lot of people – the listeners of Radio 4, perhaps.

I listened to the first episode, broadcast at 6.30 p.m., with my parents in their Surrey house. It started with a normal middle-class presenter doing a parody of *Down Your Way*. Then, static, a phantasmagoria of radio tuning – opera, foreign news and then Chantal's piping south London voice: 'A'right, listen up! Hold tight for some drainpipe-type mixing!'

And we were off.

My father looked aghast and proud, and kept cracking up. My mum laughed till she cried. I felt elated and frightened. This sort of uncharted anarchy, piping out across the green spaces of Middle England, felt surreal. I was being broadcast on the same airwaves as *The Shipping Forecast*, *Woman's Hour*, *The Archers* . . .

Doon Your Way received the second highest number

of complaints the BBC had ever experienced. I had definitely *not* set out to do this. My shock was what the complaints were about. I assumed it would be the semi-sexual content of Athene's Love Corner with her snap-fastening teddies for those luxury nights in, but the majority of complaints were from Christians about a character I played called Pippa the young Christian. There were vicious, furious letters from vicars in a crusade against Doon Mackichan.

At a conference discussing the future of radio, the *Telegraph*'s Gillian Reynolds stood up, very cross, and addressed Jonathan James Moore.

'What are you going to do about Doon Mackichan?''

It felt clear that she wanted me off air immediately. Pippa was a young idealist Christian who thought homosexuality was wrong. She sang badly rapped parables about the Prodigal Son and prostitutes, and would cite ludicrous examples to justify her point. 'Do you see stallions in the fields holding hooves? No! Because it's wrong! Wrong! Wrong!'

I loved her and so did the audience. John Peel said it was the funniest show he had ever heard on radio. The show continued to air, but the complaints rolled in. I had no idea it would cause such a furore.

One show included Single Mothers' Question

Time with Princess Diana, in which Di gave endearing but useless advice to women on council estates who couldn't afford the gas bills and whose husbands were on dialysis machines.

Di's advice would be along the lines of 'Have a stack of Florentines and a bloody good cry'.

I imagine the show was never re-aired or sold as a box set because of this one item, which, of course, after her death was utterly inappropriate. But did anyone consider re-editing it, cutting the Diana section and selling it? Sadly, no. I never pursued it, but I did pursue a TV version. A BBC producer smiled kindly and pointed to a big picture of French and Saunders on his wall. Need he say more?

Despite not getting my TV series, *Doon Your Way* had been listened to and applauded by many. The producer Armando Iannucci had seen me perform stand-up and got me into the *Mary Whitehouse* (unpleasant) *Experience*, then he asked me to join a team for a new radio show entitled *On the Hour*. Rebecca Front, Steve Coogan, Dave Schneider, Patrick Marber and I all sat around a microphone in Broadcasting House for our first improvised comedy sketch. It was a parody of *Loose Ends* (which I had scant knowledge of, so I valiantly performed some characters while feeling like an utter fraud. I completely expected to be fired before the next session). Coogan and I were the only two who hadn't been to Oxford. The banter was a bit over my head, but miraculously I stayed, and we honed our improvisational skills as a team. Then, *On the Hour* developed into a TV series, *The Day Today*.

This time, the improvisation took place in a basement in Percy Street. Armando would record our sessions on camera and then have transcripts typed up of the best bits, which we would then rehearse again. I slightly dreaded the walk down into that basement, feeling like I wasn't funny or witty enough, that I was time-wasting, that I could be recast at any time. Steve was electric with ideas.

One of my characters was Collaterlie Sisters, the business desk newsreader in *The Day Today*. For this character, I was given the script on the day, no rehearsal, lines on autocue, and I simply read it in my best newsreader's voice. I was panicking as I had no time to develop this character in improvisations. I just read the autocue. She was strict and unsmiling, and Armando told me to be like a robot that could malfunction at any time. When broadcast, she became something of a favourite but always with rather sexual overtones in the feedback and reviews. Even Coogan, in the recent episode of *The Reunion* on Radio 4, commented on the whiff of S&M about her. Should I have been flattered that I was being talked about by mostly boys and men who seemed excited and aroused? The whole question of whether women can be funny dominated much of Eighties comedy. But funny *and* sexy? It was always deemed too much.

Chris Morris was the frontman of *The Day Today*. We were his ensemble in the newsroom and for location items. It was wonderful and liberating to be improvising – once I wasn't so afraid – with a team of such great comedy actors. I got the whole series delivered one night to my flat before it aired on TV. I watched the whole lot with rising pride and disbelief at its packaged brilliance. It felt ground-breaking, iconic, seminal (all those annoying words), and there was only one series. That is class.

It's no surprise that being part of *The Day Today* helped boost all our careers. It spawned the fabulous Alan Partridge radio show, *Knowing Me, Knowing You*, where, again, we would improvise, and this would be distilled into a script from which we could stray a little during the live performances. Having been a team member of *The Day Today* helped enormously, and the show led to a *Partridge* TV commission. At the time, I was in early pregnancy with my first child, and when I was about three months pregnant, while improvising a punk singer for the show's first episode, I slipped and broke my thumb, falling hard. It was a wake-up call. I could have lost the baby. I pulled out of the series: physical comedy and pregnancy didn't really work even though other characters were more sedentary. It was agony to step away from this brilliant comedy team that everyone was talking about. I was gutted. I had already improvised a transsexual character (the part was given to Minnie Driver who wrote me a letter thanking me for such funny lines) and I did come back in a voluminous dress to hide the bump to play half a lesbian couple in 'Show Five'.

Having been forced to pull out of *Partridge*, it was a joy to get a call from Chris Morris saying that he was working on another show and could we meet up. I was becoming increasingly disillusioned with the way that crime was being reported on TV, for example in *Crimewatch* when the lighting was low and the graphics were a big thumbprint behind a perfectly coiffed and lip-glossed Fiona Bruce huskily reporting the rape of a young girl behind a church. Or the way that, in newspapers, rape was reported alongside images of topless women. So many mixed messages, blurred lines and deeply irresponsible and dangerous reporting. I couldn't have been more overjoyed therefore that the next show Chris was working on involved many of these themes.

Britain had been in the grip of a moral panic following the abduction and murder of an eight-year-old boy by a sex offender, and the press were stoking anxiety. The *News of the World* were 'naming and shaming' and implying that there was a threat around every corner.

'Paedogeddon' focused on the hysteria and the sense of vigilante justice in the air. At the time, I had two small children, and I remember the press coverage of 'a paedo on every corner'. The young mums I was spending time with, often in parks or at the swings, were buying into this scaremongering. It created a volatile and dangerous atmosphere of having to police our own children and of any lone man being a potential perpetrator. The show wanted to explore the nuances in this conversation by high-lighting and exaggerating the ridiculous lengths people were going to – paediatricians' windows being smashed as people had misunderstood the word, a man roaming the streets dressed as a school, Chris Morris keeping his own child in a filing cabinet in his office for safety. It was amazingly liberating to perform, because the subject matter was very close to my heart and something I still campaign about (for instance, the years-long campaign to have No More Page 3, which eventually succeeded).

The show aired and all hell broke loose. I was doorstepped the day after it went out by the *Daily Mail*. A nice middle-aged woman was actually standing on my doorstep. I thought she may have been a neighbour wanting some sugar, but she was wondering if, as a mother, and a woman, I had 'any comment on the furore surrounding this programme'.

It took a minute to sink in. My children were standing next to me. Someone behind her had a camera. I shut the door. The next day, I was blanked in the playground and my local beautician's refused to see me, saying they were fully booked. Then, soon after, a double-page spread in the *Mail* featured a huge, grotesque picture of me throwing my head back and laughing, with the caption, 'Mackichan laughing at the suffering of children'. I was forced to stay indoors for a week.

Out of context, the show looked bad. People had read transcripts in the papers and made their decision without watching the show. Phrases like, 'Well, if you think paedophilia is funny, then I feel sorry for you,' were par for the course.

The knee-jerk reaction from the press was a damaging and eviscerating character assassination, along the lines of: 'Her career has faltered compared to her *Day Today* peers, so she needed something like this base shock value to reignite it.' I tried my best not to read the coverage. They even contacted my mother in Spain on her landline asking for a quote. She said something like, 'Oh, but she loves children! I bet she regrets this terribly.'

Despite the huge and emotional journey the show took me on, and the continuing shockwaves of people's reactions to it, I am proud of the show and its message. It was a heady, timely, political piece of TV that really struck a note. From being the 'feed' and playing roles that didn't satisfy my desire to create change with my work, the *Brass Eye* special had the right synergy of politics and comedy that my early stand-up had been about, but which had been repressed over time. I was finally in something that I totally believed in. I had been the presenter of what was later deemed to be the most shocking TV show of all time.

Nine

The Trailblazer

Casting Call

Actress wanted to appear in an all-female comedy show. Requires experienced and versatile actress to play multiple characters in a groundbreaking sketch show: writer, performer and improviser. We are looking for unique and talented women who have 'funny bones'. The show will have no catchphrases and no repeat characters so comic invention is essential.

I was living in a council estate in Brixton when I met an author called Martin Millar at an anti-David Alton abortion bill march and benefit that I was performing at. We hit it off. He wrote an article

81

on me for *The Face* magazine, and I then read all his brilliant novels. We had a mutual love of Jane Austen, *Emma* being our favourite. We began adapting it for the theatre, with the naïve thought that we might get funding from somewhere and perform it in the Arches at Loughborough Junction near to where we lived. We met once a week at the Brixton Brasserie to work on it, filled in various applications, but didn't get funding. The script lay on a shelf for eight years until a friend said that the East Dulwich Tavern were doing a play-reading and the scout was looking for Edinburgh shows for the Gilded Balloon. I took down *Emma*, reread it and was surprised at its vitality and modernity. It was a joy to cast – eight women and one man. I could put all my brilliant actor friends in it, direct it and, of course, play Emma.

The night before the read-through, after a mere day's rehearsal, I went to an awards ceremony with Steve Coogan and Armando for *I'm Alan Partridge*. Armando told me there was a pilot for an all-female sketch show and asked if I was interested. One of the actresses had pulled out. I shilly-shallied in a grumpy way as I had pitched an all-female sketch show a year before and been rebuffed. Strangely, it was the same producer. Armando thought it was funny. I was unsure. He pushed. I agreed to watch it, and the VHS of the pilot was delivered on the morning of the *Emma* read-through. (The production went to Edinburgh Festival that summer, had successful runs at the Tricycle and Watford theatres, and was published. But I digress.)

I didn't watch the *Smack the Pony* pilot until midnight – and very nearly didn't watch it at all. I was still annoyed that my own sketch show had been turned down and I was excited about my new theatre project. I had been told that I needed to decide by the next morning or the role would be offered to another actress.

So, a bit drunk and very late, promising myself I'd watch five minutes, I started playing the tape on my little yellow TV, with its video slot underneath. I watched Sally Phillips as a lonely traffic warden, trying to gatecrash various funerals by blagging that she knew the deceased. I loved it. It was different; no punchlines, great female characters – not feeds but complicated, messy, imperfect women – and had something I had pitched in my own show a year before: video diaries of women looking for love, strong female characters, clowning and sexual politics. It felt like karma. Some parts of the show had been my idea and had finally come back to me. I said yes. After a run of *Emma* at the Gilded Balloon in Edinburgh, I would begin the first series of *Smack the Pony* in the autumn.

When rehearsals for *Emma* began, we were performing with the bare minimum of props and costumes. The women wore Empire line dresses with culottes underneath (to allow for handstands, of course.) A trunk of dressing-up clothes served to denote certain characters. There were two benches, and a beautifully painted map of the Woodhouses' locality was our backdrop. I was more than happy with our production. It was dark, funny, subversive and very fast.

We put Jane Austen on stage with her rather wild and rather irrepressible nieces, whom she often got to perform her books aloud once they were completed, and gave her the leading male role of Mr Knightley while the nieces squabbled over who would play the other roles. So, the main love story between Knightley and Emma was played out by two women, and it worked like a dream.

We performed the show for three weeks to brilliant reviews. 'Ebullient and mischievous' *The Times*, 'Full of life and vitality – an admirably lively, daringly provocative adaptation' *The Telegraph*. We had an insane five-minute get-out and get-in to the theatre.

We all got changed in a toilet and the audience loved it. It was offered a run at the Tricycle Theatre, then at Watford Theatre and, joy of joys, it was published by Nick Hern Books. It is now the staple of small rep theatres and amateur dramatic groups. I've seen four productions of it, and I am immensely proud of what started as a mutual love of *Emma* by two twenty-five-year-old strangers still being performed and offering wonderful roles for eight women.

How did I raise the money for this? I swam the Channel, of course, but more of that anon.

After watching the pilot of *Smack the Pony*, I was in. I was excited and nervous, but had no real expectations as to the future of the show. I didn't know the other performers; at this point, it was just another 'comedy job', but this time, mercifully, and oh so rarely, we were all women. We had a rather excruciating meet-and-greet just off Percy Street – Sally Phillips, Fiona Allen and me, with assorted producers, execs and directors. Sally was like a bouncing puppy dog, brimming with ideas and shouting with laughter, effusive and mercurial. Fiona seemed more reserved, didn't crack much of a smile and pretty much ignored me. I later found out that she thought the casting was bad in that we were both skinny and had long brown hair. In her eyes, we looked too similar. The harder I tried with her, the worse it got. I thought I could never be funny in that atmosphere. I was also exhausted with two small children at home while the others were still child-free, so I found the early days a struggle. Up all night with a vomiting child, then a punishing fourteen-hour day in a freezing field shooting a pop video and trying to come up with comic ideas. Sometimes I demanded time off for a parents' evening or sports day, but it wasn't always granted, so brought the children in I did and even had them in some of our sketches.

We had a sort of manifesto for our house style and content. No jokes that were 'women's issues', so nothing about diets, periods, women obsessed with chocolate, no overt sexual politics, no repeat characters and no punchlines. In short, we had our work cut out. The format would be longer sketches intercut with quickies (very short sketches) and video dates – a smorgasbord of female characters looking for love – and we would always end with a song. This caused some disagreement at first. Were the songs to be good, bad, parodies? It all felt a bit 'Light Entertainment'. Surely we were provocateurs, comedy rebels? But when we improvised the first song, where we were all playing instruments in a field or a hay barn singing about sometimes being a horse, it was so silly but very funny that we kept on with it.

The pop videos were genre parodies rather than particular bands – indie music, folk, techno, rock. There was a Manchester band quite close to Oasis where we all played men, a ludicrous techno song 'I Just Can't Find My Friend' and a country and western-style song 'I'm Really Interesting'. We would often work right up to the wire with ideas – our producer must have despaired, but last-minute solutions found on the day were often the best: using a random prop on a set, changing a character trait.

We had our manifesto and a stack of rejected sketches from (mostly male) writers who had sent them to Rory Bremner, Mel and Griff, Fry and Laurie – basically any male comic who was on TV. We dumped a lot of these sketches but kept a few, subverting expectations to make the characters female instead of male and, crucially, making the feed the funny one. We had all spent years being the feed in men's shows. This was payback time. We were *very* good at being the straight one (providing the line before the punchline), but the straight in our show soon became the funny one. And, of course, we got rid of the punchlines; at the end of the sketch the camera would wander off, dispensing with the quick ejaculation of a punchline and allowing the orgasm to go on and on.

We would rework a sketch we had chosen, often for the whole day, discarding punchlines and deepening characters.

Two bomb disposal experts
Two car mechanics
Two doctors
Two scientists
Two office workers
Two men at a bar

Once we'd picked our favourites to rework, we submitted our own sketches, and then it was our producer's tricky job of saying yes or no. We also used a camera to film improvisations, a technique we had used in *The Day Today*. Often an improvisation would have us in hysterics, but we hadn't filmed or written it down, and the next day it had just evaporated. So many bubbles burst. There were hours and hours of improvisation. We worked mostly in a rehearsal space just off Tottenham Court Road, with an overpowering smell of stale soup and toilet bleach, and outside the frosted glass a permanent, shuffling, coughing line of people queuing up for their lunch at the American Church.

For the first hour or two of a typical day's rehearsal, we would catch up, talk about what had been happening to us, our relationships, my kids. These sessions were gold dust, where the real truth of the female experience was examined from all sides and then formed into a sketch. It also led to some of our most outlandish work (a pole dancing class I had once done turned into a routine of a woman with shopping bags lap-dancing a lamppost). But sometimes it took painful hours, or days, to find what the hook was. Was it too 'comedy', too 'arch'? Too 'obvious'? Too 'tub-thumping'? Too 'sad'?

I don't know how many weeks we spent in that basement (it felt like years) with the homeless shuffling past the windows. The frustration when something worked so well the day before but seemed excruciating the next. Months later, with several different writers in the room and many, many pages discarded, the sudden joy of a brilliant sketch made the writing feel magical. Laughter can dissolve enmity, jealousy and fear. Fiona and I were put together in sketches, and it worked, and she seemed to thaw. In fact, we started to gel, comedically and socially. I am not particularly competitive, and we all had our different strengths and weaknesses – Sally, a brilliant, funny girl, with mischief in her eyes, a classic clown. Fiona, deadpan naturalism queen, multi-accented; and me, gangly clown, unafraid of looking really ugly and mostly falling over.

Often, the sketches we released were funny in the main body of them: the idea, the character and not the punchline. By binning the punchlines, we improvised scenes where there was no ending. This was pretty radical. We had a sort of trust that when we filmed we would find something on the day. We rehearsed and re-rehearsed and over-rehearsed what we had. We had a stack of video dates that we divided up but didn't rehearse until the day. Finally, we were 'ready'. We had our six half-hour scripts.

Most of the series was filmed on location, in various offices, schools and pavements, and we all shared a caravan. On a filming day, once out of make-up and in costume we would run and rerun lines and then typically have a new idea and drag the producer, Vicky Pile, in to try it out.

Changes on the day were nerve-racking. Sometimes we had just over-rehearsed and got bored; sometimes we needed to stick to the original; but equally comedy gold could turn up in the moment via a prop, a new character idea, a different wig, anything. It was vital, fluid and constantly changing. In each series, that caravan became our home for six weeks, with our individual lives, our joys and woes, our relationships and, at the time, my children, all shared while making comedy. Make-up had to be redone, sometimes because of tears of laughter, and we supported and egged each other on. We had to.

The very first day of filming, we began with a sketch of me doing an expert limbering up, poolside, the image of a proper athlete, all laser-like focus, before a fabulous belly flop and flailing doggy paddle. The next sketch was two women walking their dogs who turn and bark at each other.

Nobody laughed.

The crew remained stony-faced. We were convinced the show was a disaster and reinforced the message we'd been told for years – that we just weren't funny. The filming felt painful at times. We would run back into our caravans and scream with embarrassment. The crew looked bored or bewildered. The cameramen would just drift away from us at the end of a sketch. We buoyed each other up as no one else was. There were tears and panic attacks. (I had one filming a sketch on horseback when I was paralysed with fright. I had had a bad fall from a horse and I ended up sobbing, unable to film.) We were constantly running back to make-up and costume as there were so many character changes and often the voice would come as soon as the wig was on. We would do a quick try-out in front of each other and our feedback was genuine and allowed us to fail and to fly. We were exhausted and genuinely thought it was mediocre at best, probably a bit of a flop. I truly don't think we would have persevered were it not for all of us trying to lift one another up.

At the end of the shoot, having run out of time, we were forced to film all the incidental video diaries in under a day, running in and out of wigs and make-up and then running back, keeping the kettle boiling. An insane afternoon of perhaps fifteen characters each, often ones we'd never rehearsed and looks we had never seen. The speed proved to be its joy. The video clips were full of pauses and real naturalism of fumbling and desperation. They remain some of the most sublime bits of comedy and some of my favourite bits of the show. We had to look straight down the lens, but I clearly remember we were back from location and in a studio, and I could see from the corner of my eye a line of male silhouettes and most of the shoulders were shaking with laughter. Maybe it *was* funny? Maybe bits of it would work?

Before the final edit, the first three episodes were shown to a studio audience at the BBC and the laughter was recorded and played very low-level in the episodes. The sketches that didn't get laughed at were scrapped. We stood at the back, hiding in a state of ecstasy. People were laughing. We laughed at everything, often more at the scenes that were cut because they were too obscure or surreal, but cuts had to be made and, wonder of wonders, it was funny. It had been expertly packaged, graded, edited and, in a way, styled. It had its own 'house style'. I had no idea at the time about long lenses or colour washes, but the whole look and feel was vibrant, anarchic and different.

Episode one aired. I watched it with a few friends in our rented flat in Clapham with a growing joy. It did work. There were no mobiles then, of course, but the landline rang during the ad break and then didn't stop for the rest of the evening. The reviews were brilliant. We all took a deep breath.

During the making of series two, we were informed that an up-and-coming comic called Ricky Gervais wanted to come in and talk to us about some ideas he had had. We asked him to send in any material he wanted, but he wouldn't. He wanted to meet us in person. We politely declined and carried on with our improvisation sessions. Another request came to meet, another polite refusal. Then, one morning, our producer said he had found out where we were rehearsing and had come to the door. He was outside. Being good girls, we thought we couldn't continue ignoring him and we'd better let him in. He entered, all smiles and confidence, and took over the room, basically giving us ideas that placed him in the centre and us as his feeds. He believed that with him involved – and, naturally, front and centre – the show would definitely reach new heights. He knew it was an all-female sketch show, albeit with the hugely talented Darren Boyd and Cavan Clerkin providing supporting male roles when we needed them. He had literally landed from Planet Ego and tried to get us to go along with his plan for our show. Again, we politely declined.

One saddening but, I suppose, to-be-expected result of a successful female-led show was that word on the street was that we all hated each other. Chinese whispers abounded: we had all fallen out, it was a toxic atmosphere, it was deeply competitive and so on. Many times, when we were questioned about how we got on, there were sceptical, raised eyebrows when we said we thrived together, recognised each other's skills and were supportive. The reporters didn't really believe us. We were obviously covering something up. We couldn't be funny, talented, original *and* still remain friends. It was too much for them to comprehend. They wouldn't have it. Often when men write for women they write 'bitches', basically setting women up against each other. In our show, we had women being competitive but physically: drinking bigger and bigger bottles of water, using bigger and bigger thongs as braces. But we ditched the 'bitch' and had real women on screen. This was pretty revolutionary.

Asked once by a famous artist why I didn't think *Smack the Pony* was recommissioned when we tried a few years later for a *Smack Two*, I said that I didn't think the female clown was allowed to be sexy as well as funny. It's something I have come up against time and time again. He sarcastically replied, mock-crying, 'Oooh, boo hoo! I'm sexy and funny! Nobody wants me! Poor little me!'

This was not at all what I was saying. It is just perhaps that this sort of female clown is too empowered. A fat clown – yes, we can tolerate. A stupid clown – yes, we'll laugh at her. A nympho clown – yes. A desperate clown – sure. But intelligent? Sexy? Hmm, don't see so many of those.

The first time I ever met this artist, at a London

gallery, he shimmied over to me and said, 'Doon Mackichan, I had a very filthy dream about you a few weeks ago.'

But he was dressed as a woman . . . so I suppose that was all right. Once again, the wind was well and truly taken out of my sails. I was flabbergasted, and felt awkward and ashamed. Somehow as women we are repeatedly punished for daring to be brave and taking risks with our work. So we have to be doubly fearless to keep creating in this climate.

Some years after the last series, Fiona, Sally and I got together, this time with nine children between us and several family storms along the way, and looked at the possibility of a *Smack the Pony* reunion, or something that involved the three of us. We had meetings, we wrote some great sketches, this time for 'older' women, but it just never happened and kept never happening despite our pushing. Why? Because we were older? We would never know.

Smack the Pony was a trailblazing show. There had never been an all-female sketch show like it. There had rarely been a comedy show without repeat characters, catchphrases or, indeed, punchlines. But the wonderfully silly synergy of women being allowed free rein was liberating. To suck a glass onto your face in a pub, then quietly try to pull it off, while your friend tells you a tragic relationship story. Huge, wispy pubes showing in a swimming-pool changing room. A woman holding on to a man's leg being dragged along the floor of a dancefloor, club and airport. A lot of falling in water. There is not a great history of female clowns and we righted that. But look at what came after. A raft of female-led shows? Less stereotyped roles for women in comedy? A sea change? It has taken years for more female-led shows to be ruling the screens but it is slowly happening.

For years, we didn't make it onto any lists of the 'Top 100 Funniest Shows Ever' or 'Ten Most Seminal Comedy Shows'. We had received two Emmys in New York and countless international awards (Golden Rose of Montreux), but no recognition in Britain. For decades, the UK lists have been largely male-dominated – *Monty Python*, *Morecambe and Wise*, the *Carry On* films, *Benny Hill*, *Fry and Laurie*, *Fawlty Towers*, *The Armando Ianucci Shows*, *The Brian Conley Show*, Mitchell and Webb, Armstrong and Miller, Baddiel and Skinner, Harry Hill, the list goes on! We have just recently sneaked onto the list, like a vintage homage; maybe the show is less disturbing now that it's twenty years on. But are women in comedy equal to men? No. We're still in the (very) Dark Ages. Panel shows, comedy films, sketch shows, stand-ups. It's the funny man who is still considered solid ground. But it is changing slowly.

After all our success and millions and millions of YouTube hits, there *Smack the Pony* stays. It is still what most people love from my work. It is still inspiring young women and, hopefully, men too. The women I meet now who were inspired to pursue their careers of directing, writing, acting and producing were watching *Smack the Pony* aged ten and are now the women I am working with. That is an utter joy. I was 'fangirled' recently by a famous director who said the reason she started was *Smack the Pony*, and a wonderful shop owner in Margate told me she had started her shop A Little Bit of Happy because of us. So, yes, the legacy still ripples out.

Ten

The Selkie

Casting Call

Amazonian, strong, lithe and beautiful heroine* required for our still-developing adventure film. The storyline will feature one of the following:

a) Climbing Everest

b) Swimming the Channel, or

c) Rowing the Atlantic

*Please note that we reserve the right to recast as a man.

Actors are often asked in their early careers to work for 'free' – even if expenses are paid. The producer of *Emma* in Edinburgh had agreed to pay for the venue, the publicity and our accommodation, no small input, and one for which I am eternally grateful (she had heard rave reviews from the East Dulwich Tavern). But despite her generosity, it still meant the actors not taking home a wage for a month's rehearsal and three weeks' performance at the festival. I racked my brain to think of a way to pay the actors (this was pre-crowdfunding) and I struck gold when I met an actress who said she was available for the run in Edinburgh but needed a weekend off in the middle to 'swim the Channel'.

By coincidence I had just finished reading an incredible memoir about an American scene designer who lived in New York and decided she wanted to swim the English Channel. Sally Friedman had been obsessed with the idea since her youth, and her husband supported her training by kayaking next to her as she attempted longer and longer swims in huge lakes outside New York. She spent months swimming in ever colder water to prepare and reading everything about the crossing. When she was fully trained, Friedman hired a boat and a captain.

Each summer in a week's window in August about three hundred people attempt to cross the Channel: some solo, some in pairs, some in relay groups of six. Friedman had an allotted slot, had paid her entrance fee and the flights for her and her husband, and excitement mounted. Then, the evening before she was due to fly to Britain, her husband was killed by a bus in Manhattan. Felled by grief and shock, she lay awake the whole night, and decided to do the swim for him. She made it to Dover, where she sat on the beach and realised that she couldn't do it. She sat and sobbed, then flew back home.

Grief, salt water, tears, the sea, love, pushing yourself to the limit. It was a powerful story, and although I had always loved swimming I had never wanted to compete in any way or endurance-swim. For me it was a solitary, meditative time, a balm for the soul in the miracle of water. But I was smitten by this story.

I babbled about this incredible book I had just read and asked this actress everything about her upcoming swim. She was doing a six-person relay with three paratroopers and two friends, crossing on 1 August, and they were training in Tooting Lido and the sea. I was desperately trying to find a way to raise money to pay my actors. I thought I could perhaps be in the boat and somehow raise money that way; it was all very hazy and vague, but the long and short of it is, I joined her for the training at the lido one utterly freezing morning in early April and every day thereafter we stayed in longer and longer. I began to love the cold water. It gave me energy and banished the demons, and before I knew it I was on the team as a substitute. As the swim date grew nearer, one of the team got an ear infection and the coach decided we couldn't risk it. We were only as good as our weakest swimmer and I was officially a team member. I was going to swim the Channel on 1 August in a relay. What had started as a publicity stunt ended up as a Channel swim. The training was helping me cope with my personal life upheavals – two small children, financial worries. I wanted to keep fighting for my family and thought this might help me to build resilience.

While all the other swimmers swam for the British Heart Foundation or Cancer Research, I was swimming to take a play I'd co-created to Edinburgh – an arts charity, I suppose. And why not?

We trained for four months, April to July, swimming up to an hour in the warming water every day, and we had to complete six sea swims in the same period. These were a lot harder, with the waves, the seaweed, the swallowing of water and cramp, but we just had to keep going. We were rarely out in the open water – the majority of our training was in open-air lidos, not heated pools – but when we did sea-swim we just crawled along a coastline very much in sight of land.

I am not a competitive sportswoman, but I got fitter and fitter – the fittest I'd ever been – and it gave me a wonderful energy. It didn't springboard me into further events (triathlons, Ironmans and so on) although I did compete in the World Ice Swimming Championships in the Arctic (that's a story in itself – perhaps for my next book). This was a one-off and I knew it. Just do it, I thought, when the training felt particularly bleak. I was pushing my endurance in the water and in life.

The numbness in my extremities lessened as the weather warmed and my routine post-swim was coming back to get the kids ready for nursery or school, and then rehearsals for *Emma* at 10 a.m. In the early days, I would often shake for two or three hours after a swim, realising I had stayed in too long. I became acutely aware of my limits and knew that when I started to feel warm I had to get out because it was the beginning of hypothermia.

As D-Day approached I had so much adrenaline. I was hopping about like a mad creature, exhausted, overexcited, a bit manic. I was banishing my fear – fear of the deep, the danger, the isolation, and the fact that I was the only mother swimming. However, I made it very clear that I would never swim in the dark.

The night before the swim in Dover we all checked in to Webb's Hotel. We were to meet in the harbour at 5.30 a.m. the next day. We didn't sleep all night. If the sea was too rough, we would have to wait until the right conditions allowed us to cross. It would be in the hands of the captain. If we missed our crossing window, we wouldn't be allowed to do it. Some Channel crossers wait weeks due to adverse weather and then it can just be cancelled. The sea gods. How I invoked them! I even had a shrine at home to all the sea witches for a safe crossing.

The next morning, the wind sounded strong. We met our teammates for an almost silent breakfast. I was terrified. No butterflies in my stomach, there were herds of drunken, fighting elephants. We carted the mountains of food down to our boat at the harbour, which we found with all the curtains closed. We knocked. We waited. The sea in the harbour looked sort of calm, but there seemed to be a powerful wind knocking all the masts in a cacophony of alarm. The minutes ticked by. We were all desperate to get started. We knocked. We shouted.

A cross, rumpled man emerged eventually from

the hatch, hungover by the looks of him. He proceeded to grunt angry orders at us as we stowed our bags and food below: twenty-five bags of high-energy food – soup, fruit, pasta.

'If you're gonna be sick, for God's sake keep upwind of me. I will only say this once. Pay attention! Everyone needs to change into dry costumes below. If you're sick below, for fuck's sake clean it up. No touching of the boat once you're in the water, or you will all be disqualified. When you're entering the water swim behind the swimmer in front and out into the water for your hour.'

We were to swim one hour on and five hours off. We motored through Dover harbour and then we hit the sea. It was rough, perhaps too rough for a crossing, but this captain didn't care. He was making hay. It seemed we were an annoying but lucrative bunch of idiots. Swimming idiots. Amateurs with our red hats, looking like angry safety matches. I wasn't enjoying being under his watch. The magnitude of the situation was beginning to dawn on us all when we were given our instructions.

'No thermals allowed. No wet suits, no gloves. Just your bog-standard swimsuit and hat.'

I tucked passport pictures of my kids under my hat. As the only mother on the team, I'd said that

I didn't want to go in after dark, as this involved putting a light stick into your goggles to be visible by the boat. I offered to be the first one in. The boat motored to Shakespeare Beach, our starting point, and then we were heading for Cap Gris Nez, the lighthouse twenty-five miles away as the crow flies, but actually, by the end of the swim, thirty-one miles as our tiny sailboat zig-zagged through the busiest shipping lane in the world.

I removed all my warm layers below deck. I think someone was already being sick up on the prow as I was duly greased up by the captain's son with a large tub of Vaseline smeared around my neck and under my arms. This was to prevent salt burn from the repeated body movements which can produce an agonising sort of terrible blister (which I later experienced).

I climbed down the steps and in I went. The boat pitched and lurched crazily, rocking in the chop, and I swam to shore feeling like an Olympian. It was 6.30 a.m. I walked onto Shakespeare Beach and waited for the signal. The captain put his arm up, then down, signalling the swim had begun. Cheers from the gang! We were off!

Like any non-sportswoman, and like the hare I am, I swam like a demon, part adrenaline, part showing off. I felt sick, excited, terrified and elated. All the team were arranged along the rails, cheering and whooping. It was a fine few minutes. The sun had come out, and we were still in relatively calm sea. I learned to roll with the waves so as to not swallow too much water, and the beautiful, carved mermaid figurehead at the prow of the boat, sun sparkling off her, the water flying from her scaly flanks, was like a talisman watching me, impassive, a slight smile on her face. These figureheads were built as icons with magical significance in the old days.

I was a dolphin. I was a mermaid. I was swimming the Channel! Well, a bit of it. And then the whooping died down and the gang turned back and I saw someone drinking tea (how dare they! I needed constant whooping). The sun went in. The boat got ahead of me. Suddenly I was breathing in ghastly diesel fumes and I began to get cold. I ploughed on at a steadier pace feeling less and less like an invincible, beautiful mermaid. Were they laughing on the boat? Why weren't they watching? On and on. I was now freezing, but I felt epic, a queen of the seas, Thetis, sea goddess.

I tried to get closer to the boat, but as it lurched and tipped in the squally waves it felt like it was going to tip on top of me, so I backed off. Then, when the diesel fumes seemed to get worse, I let the boat pull further away. But then I'd feel a dreadful pang of loneliness, like I was being left behind, alone in the big sea. I was suddenly Pip the cabin boy in *Moby-Dick*. He didn't know they were coming back for him after he'd been flipped out of the boat, chasing the whale with a coil of rope attached to the Leviathan. I had reread Melville's masterpiece in the months leading up to the swim: in those few short hours before they came back to pick him up, he went quietly mute and never spoke again. It was the infinity above and below him that sent Pip mad. Our minds can't fathom it. In anticipation, I had smeared Vaseline on my goggles before I got in so I couldn't see the deep below or think about it. I scolded myself to keep going. Do it for the team. Don't stop and have a breather. Be strong for the team. To mark our progress as swimmers, a towel would be tied to the boat railings to denote fifteen minutes had passed – two towels for thirty minutes and so on. I could see no towels on the side of the boat, and I was utterly bone-cold and could only assume those on board had forgotten the towels and I was nearing the end of my hour. At last! Some movement on the boat.

'Fifteen minutes completed, Doonie! Go, Doonie. You can do it. Wooh!'

Were they having a laugh? Was this some kind of sick joke? They had been too busy chatting and drinking tea to notice the time.

'Forty-five minutes to go. Go, Doonie! You can do it!'

Hideous, hideous deflation. Three more sets of what I had just done seemed impossible. Mental, even. I might die. I'd only done fifteen minutes. What kind of a wimp was I? Hadn't I trained for four months? How could I be so unaware of time? In Brockwell Lido I had purposefully not looked at the clock until I had counted forty lengths and then I was allowed. Everything was so controlled in the pool: the bacteria, the lanes, the waves. Here I was at the mercy of the sea, and she was having a good laugh.

Miserably, I ploughed on. It seemed the longest hour of my life, then I was being helped up the rickety steps and the second swimmer set off to more whoops and I went below shaking like a puppy with pneumonia to attempt to put on a dry costume ready for my next leg. The thought was unbearable. I felt so cold.

We'd lost sight of land. We were in the middle of

the Channel. Huge, rusty ships with Russian-looking writing all over the sides came perilously close. Sometimes I could see sailors at the prow looking down on us. Huge freight ships, Seacats, hovercrafts motored what seemed too close to us. In the water it felt so loud: the engine noise was deafening, like a thousand lawn mowers in your eardrum.

Too soon it was my turn again. The paratrooper before me had had a grim hour. Crazily, he hadn't trained in cold water, so when he hit the water he had an asthma attack, then a panic attack, but he managed not to touch the boat. That would have been curtains for the whole team. He couldn't catch his breath, and he rolled onto his back again, swearing like an angry cockroach as he swallowed water and was sick.

'Fucking . . . cunting . . . bollocking . . . fuck!'

We all tried in vain to support him.

'Just breathe! Stay on your back!' we shouted, but he kept attempting to swim, swallowing water, being sick, panicking. It was desperate and he was utterly humiliated. He lay on his back, occasionally attempting a back stroke and finally shouted up at us, 'Don't look at me!'

He was pulled on board after his hour, which, like my first leg, had felt like an age, and he exploded in anger. He shouted, full of vehement self-loathing, 'No one talk to me! Don't look at me! I've let you all down. I didn't train in cold water and now we need to make up the time. I'm a cunt. Please leave me alone. Don't talk to me!'

He got dressed, sank his head to his chest and stayed utterly still for the punishing five hours like some sort of Carthusian penance until, yes, he had to go in again. Those are the rules. I tried to talk to him, feeling so sorry for him, but he had totally shut down.

So . . . go, go, go, girls! We had to make up the time that the men had lost, otherwise we would never make it before the tide turned. My friend Lucy was the queen. Her sublimely beautiful, zen-like crawl took her through the choppy waters with a sea-witch capacity for grace. Fast, efficient, brilliant.

Just as I'd got warm, I was back in the water. Every cell was screaming *no!*, but I'd eaten a whole Toblerone in a white baguette and drunk a Red Bull. The sea could not be read. There was no rhythm to its choppiness. One minute you were being carried along on the breast of a big swell, the next minute you were smacked in the face and swallowing huge mouthfuls of salt. It required a giving in, a relinquishing of goals, or speed, except just to move forward, to roll with the waves. This was the only way forward. A valuable lesson in life: it may sound like a cliché, but just roll with it. A long, wet solitary hour followed, arms beating time, singing mad nursery rhymes, then a sudden, joyful minute of complete synchronicity with the sea, the currents, the swell, the mind finally stilling, a sort of self-hypnosis.

Each of us were in our own world, trying to get warm, trying to not dread the next immersion. Incredibly, it got colder with each swim. The captain was keeping us up to date with other swimmers. 'An American bird's just been pulled from the water with hypothermia two miles from the finish.'

During one of my swims a piece of driftwood knocked my leg and I screamed, but not wanting to upset the team, I just kept screaming but only when my face was underwater. My whole body was rigid with fear and panic, the captain clocked it and just raised his index finger very slowly, denoting 'Keep it together. Relax. You can't keep swimming with that tension'. It was a monumental effort to banish the thoughts and fears of the deep – it took every ounce of energy to will myself to relax, when all I wanted to do was scramble back on deck. The sun blazed out for a rare few seconds, I could suddenly see how deep the sea was, and a swoon of vertigo hit me. But I knew I had to 'get a grip', so I smeared my goggles with Vaseline from under my armpits and swam the fuck on. Meanwhile, the humiliated army cockroach, during his swims, continued to lie on his back, swearing, and then going into mortified isolation on deck, the other paratrooper continued being sick and making little progress, and the girls were saving the day.

My last swim was at dusk. France seemed to be looming. Everyone thought this could be the last leg, and I was going very fast, pushing myself on, on, on, for the final burst. The cliffs seemed tantalisingly close after the sea-blindness. Very tangible, very high, very treacherous. I gave it everything, but unfortunately the tide was against us. The cliffs stayed where they were, and I was making little progress, almost swimming on the spot. So deflating.

I got out as it was dark, bitterly disappointed. We weren't closer, and our next swimmer went in, panicking, as in the dark it felt the boat was capsizing onto her. She felt disoriented and afraid. Lucy, our heroine, went in with her to keep her morale up and stop her panic from escalating. Again, because of the tide, they made little progress, so the captain motored a small way parallel to the coast to find an easier route for the swimmers to get to the rocks and a more hospitable landing site for us to reach the rocks.

The French Coastguard shone a light from the lighthouse to our boat, so there was a choppy, silvered river of light. Our captain shone a huge light from our boat towards the cliffs. It was decided that we would all go in for this last leg, minus the paratroopers, but the rule was that we had to climb onto the rocks to shore and clear the water. It was rough, and sudden rocks emerged which made it treacherous. There was a tiny cheer and a swim back to the boat. All told, it had taken sixteen and a half hours. We had a quick glug of bubbles, I cried talking to my kids, and then everyone found a spot on deck, doubled up and went to sleep! I sat at the mast, exhausted, freezing, but awash with a huge sense of achievement. I was delirious, hallucinating huge ships ahead of us and shouting back to the captain. We motored back to Dover with the ghost spectres of enormous ships looming ahead of us.

At home, after the swim, I lay next to my husband in bed, still in all my clothes, and cried slow, hot tears of relief and exhaustion. In the morning, I peeled myself out of my many layers, had a brandy, a hot shower and another cry; I couldn't walk without falling over.

I vowed never to do anything like that ever again. No mountains, no lakes, no heroics. No more feats of daring for me! No more heroics, thank you! I'm fine as I am. I've done it. I've swum the Channel. To this day, it remains one of the most challenging things I have ever done.

Shortly after crossing the Channel, I began work on a screenplay about three recovering addicts who meet at a rehab centre in the countryside and decide to swim the Channel as a way of reclaiming ownership of their bodies. Very different women, different classes. It took me over a year and was picked up by a TV company who wanted it as a series. But I reverted the rights when it started going in a direction I didn't like. It then went to Richard Curtis, and he absolutely loved it. He was taking it to Working Title. It was the best thing he'd read in years, he said, but then a rival director started production on a story about an unemployed man swimming the Channel, and Working Title did not want to get into battle, so it was dropped. It was suggested I go and meet the head of the TV company anyway and 'flutter my eyelashes' in a bid to persuade him to see my series through. I didn't. Was he being ironic? Perhaps. But the male hero story won the day.

Swimming the Channel is associated with a male

hero. Captain Matthew Webb was the first man to do it in 1875 (in twenty-one hours and forty minutes). He went on to challenge himself to more extreme endeavours, until he drowned attempting to swim through the whirlpool rapids beneath the Niagara Falls.

In August 1926, twenty-year-old American Gertrude Ederle became the first woman to swim the Channel (fourteen hours and thirty-four minutes). When she returned home, over two million people showed up in Manhattan to celebrate her achievement, yet no one remembers her today. Women are now equal or better than their male contemporaries, being, on average, thirty-three minutes faster, but we are very short of female hero stories in our culture.

Eleven

The Hot Lesbian

Casting Call
Domineering, no-nonsense, and a bit of
a ball-breaker, Sue is surprisingly
attractive for such a strong woman.
Head of her design company, she is gay
but hides this to improve her career
chances. Sassy and ballsy, late thirties,
slim but strong.

One of the video dates in *Smack the Pony* involved two lesbians asking for a man to join them to watch their lovemaking – to be passive or active, they didn't mind – and to teach them to pleasure him, before both declaring in a deflated way after some time, 'I don't think it's going to work.'

The joke is obviously that two women together

having sex is a bona fide male fantasy and a lot of pornography focuses on girl-on-girl action, so when I was asked to play a gay woman in a thriller alongside an ITV golden boy, I had immediate reservations about the titillating nature of a gay relationship onscreen in a show from the male gaze. I was not as sensitised to how the crime thriller genre bleeds into our culture and can fuel male violence against women in our society – at the time, I was more concerned with how to put food on the table. I had decided to stay at home for a while to see more of the children, but money was tight. And this role was offering a lot of money for a short filming period. Another draw was that a dear friend of mine – now sadly passed from breast cancer – was playing the other gay woman, so we decided we would have a laugh and make the best of it.

In this drama you didn't see any outright violence and we had a fairly silly storyline that made us howl with laughter – stage directions said 'the women kiss in the pool and disappear under the water . . . the women kiss in the sauna . . . etc'. We saw such instructions as classic stereotypes that we would inhabit as best we could, but in hindsight this should have been my first clue to the friction that would follow. In the audition, I made it crystal clear that

I was not happy with any nudity. Sadly, I can't remember if I was asked first by the director or if I volunteered this particular demand of mine, but nudity was definitely out in my books. It felt gratuitous – I felt that the message could still be conveyed without us having to put our bodies on display.

My co-star and I were up first to film our swimming-pool scene. It required a few takes because we got the giggles so much. As usual, there was a predominantly male crew witnessing these two hot thirty-somethings having a snog. We tried to laugh our way through our awkwardness – they wanted a serious sexy kiss, and we kept exploding with laughter. The crew just rolled their eyes as our shoulders just kept shaking. I was beginning to find the director creepy: he had wanted to inspect what bathing suits we were wearing, obviously wanting them to be as revealing as possible.

Then came the sauna scene. We were to be naked under our towels. No swimsuits and very tiny towels . . . thanks again to the artistic vision of the director. Happily, it is now standard practice to involve an intimacy coach for sensitive scenes, to allay any discomfort and ensure the actors feel supported. But at the time, there was no such thing, and we went with it – who knows, maybe bare shoulders and a lot of leg were essential to the story arc. After too many close-ups, being asked to repeat the scene several times with small variations – can you hold the kiss for longer? how about massaging the back of her neck? – the director drew me to one side. He asked me to drop the towel in the next take just as I exit. When I politely asked why, he claimed that it added 'authenticity'. You don't need to drop it until the very end of the scene, he tells me, just as I exit the sauna.

'Don't worry', he says. 'No one will see anything.'

'So why do it?' I ask.

This moment of the exchange is where it typically gets uncomfortable for actresses, especially if she's young and inexperienced. On the one hand, you don't want to draw unnecessary attention to yourself and cause a scene – and you know that any delays will be costing the production money – but nor do you want to transgress your own boundaries or be put into an exposing situation. You don't want to be 'the awkward prude'. What's the big deal? By this point, the male crew are getting bored and the director cajoles and cajoles. *I'm a nice guy, it would really help my shot, why are you being like this?* He's waiting for the actress to come to her senses, he has the overall vision for the piece and his vision is 'DROP THE TOWEL!' I was starting to sweat for real and nearly gave in to keep the peace. No one wants to be seen as the aforementioned 'awkward prude'. But I held my ground as the minutes ticked by, the director imploring, wheedling, pushing. Me trying to keep it light, smiling throughout. 'No, thanks. I just don't feel comfortable.' Internally, I felt as though the shoot was descending into soft porn masquerading as a crime thriller.

Then he got stroppy. He looked severely disappointed when I still refused. I wondered whether I would get sacked. Was there time to recast? Reshoot? A cold, sour wind blew in. Looking back now, I am so proud I held my ground, despite the terrible awkwardness of a whole crew waiting and the deep disapproval of the director. If I had given in to his vision, anyone, at any time, would be able to look at my breasts in a middling ITV crime drama with huge ratings.

Any publication could use it, exploit it, tamper with the image, and continue sending it round and round with all the humiliation that would involve. So many actresses I know who decided to get naked for a project have then found their images stolen and exploited and have experienced untold pain and shame. I am not ashamed of my body in any way. I will happily get my kit off for a radical feminist agenda. But gratuitous shots of naked women are everywhere on our screens while the men remain clothed. Very rarely do we see a buttock! We don't see it, as it would make men feel uncomfortable – both those in it and those watching it.

My friend, unfortunately, did not specify no nudity, and in her storyline her character was later brutally murdered (thankfully, we did not see this play out on screen), but she was most definitely in full view on the slab. I did not know she was to be nude on the slab; in the script it only said 'body bag'.

I remember sitting with my fellow actress and dear friend in a freezing cold room holding her hand while the make-up lady covered her bare breasts and torso in stab wounds, blood and mud. I told her she could change her mind, but she said it was too late, the contract was signed. I wanted her to fight, but she didn't, as it had been agreed in her contract, so instead, she quietly cried as the make-up went on, the scars and bruises – it was traumatic.

There is no way on earth I would have said yes to this job a few years later: a virtually all-male crew, a male director and a male lead, especially consid-

ering the degrading and disheartening amount of
'crime porn' on TV. But I didn't watch much TV
back then and was not as aware. Now, I campaign
to stop the endless 'dead female' dramas, which
seem to me to stoke a vile appetite for rape as
entertainment plots.

Roughly a year ago, I was offered a part in a
major crime drama for money I could not afford to
turn down (post-pandemic and the joys of Universal
Credit). The offer email said, after cataloguing the
actors who had been involved in it, how marvellous
it would be to have me on board.

'We wanted to flag up now, like with most characters that die in the show, Doon will be seen on
the slab as dead for a post-mortem, so we can talk
about what that looks like, and what she/you would
be comfortable with.'

I took great pleasure in turning this part down
while sending the casting director a link to my *Body
Count Rising* documentary for Radio 4. I wonder if
they listened, I wonder if they laughed, I wonder
if they felt angry or self-righteous. In my documentary I look at how our entertainment is dominated
by women as victims, either being chased, assaulted,
raped or dead on the slab, and these shows are very
much on the rise. Sadly, I was part of one that did

exactly this. I now campaign against them, and urge actors and actresses I know not to become involved. It feeds a culture that is killing us. Life mirrors art mirrors life. This sort of television is traumatic for women and titillating to the wrong sort of men.

Twelve

The Deranged Mother

Casting Call
Actress in her early forties wanted to play mother of a son who contracts leukaemia, aged nine. She will be required to play a huge range of emotions — grief, rage, denial and hysteria — so heavyweight actress needed at the top of her game. The twist at the end of the story is that it isn't a drama, it's real life and involves a two-year commitment, shooting mostly at a children's cancer ward in Surrey.

I am forty-one, India is ten years old, Louis is nine, and my second daughter Ella is one (born at home in water despite all the grave misgivings of doctors as I am a 'geriatric' mother!).

I had been involved in developing a sitcom, a two-hander with the brilliant Michelle Gomez, written by the equally brilliant Georgia Pritchett, and to our shared delight it was commissioned after a group of execs had watched a workshop of episode one. It was a comedy police double act with much physical humour – female leads and a female writer and producer. Hurrah!

I was just about to decamp to Scotland with my nanny and one-year-old for a six-week short sitcom – to my relief the baby very much welcomed in this all-female team. It was to be a lovely Christmas at home then departure in January.

My son Louis, an avid footballer and captain of his primary school team, had started complaining that his feet hurt. We assumed it was just too much football, so we kept him off for a few days. Then, his fingers swelled up, so we took him for a routine GP check-up. They took blood. We didn't hear anything, but I kept a cautious eye over him. A few days later, on Christmas Eve, we were told they wanted to admit him to King's College Hospital. They'd identified something called vasculitis and needed to give him intravenous antibiotics. Amid the chaos of Christmas and family plans we suddenly found ourselves on a ward, full of disbelief.

I was given a cot next to him, and on Christmas morning he was given a wrapped present by the staff. To our great joy, on Boxing Day we were discharged, and headed for our family Christmas in Hastings with my brother and his family. After a two-day hiatus, everything was back to normal. There was snow. Louis didn't want to join in with the old carols around the piano, but we just thought he was tired and grumpy after the strong antibiotics and injections. He was very pale and constantly exhausted.

After the holidays he was still not himself, so we kept him off school. I enjoyed a sort of stolen time with him, like a secret holiday. Towards the end of the week, he still looked pale, so I vowed I would take him back to the doctor's the next morning. While unloading logs from the car, with Louis next to me, my husband, who was inside on the phone, began gesticulating for me to come into the house. When he finishes the call, he tells me that Louis has been diagnosed with acute myeloid leukaemia and we need to pack a bag immediately and get to the hospital. I, of course, ask what his chance of survival is, but they don't give that information over the phone so we need to go quickly. I go to his room and pack chaotically. Man United pillowcase. New trainers. Pyjamas, a *Simpsons* comic. I seem stuck, kneeling on his bedroom floor. Magic tricks?

My husband bellows, 'Hurry up!'

The doctor explains things we don't understand when we get to King's College. We are told Louis has something called 'blast cells' in his blood. The soles of his feet have large red spots on them that the doctor had drawn on a diagram. Why didn't we see that? He needs to start treatment urgently. They're trying to find him a place in the hospital. They have calls out to Great Ormond Street and the Royal Marsden. We later find out, had his treatment not started he would have been dead in two weeks. My brain refuses to compute such information.

A place is found at the Royal Marsden in Sutton. He is taken by ambulance. I go home to collect more clothes.

At home, I fall onto the kitchen floor and sob. They can't say exactly how long he'll be in the hospital, but we're told it will be a matter of months. I suddenly can't drive – my body's in shock. I take a cab to the hospital, feeling a huge panic. Louis is sitting in a corner bay on his hospital bed. He is so white his skin looks translucent, like all the other children in that ward. Why didn't I see that? I berate myself with an intensely critical inner monologue. What sort of a mother am I? I'm expecting a doctor to call out my name and tell me in an authoritative, without-a-shadow-of-a-doubt voice, 'There's been a terrible mistake! So sorry. You can go home.'

My mind is still contorting ways to get out. Should we seek a second opinion? Could there be a mix-up? How could I get him out? We can't stay here. It's denial. We fill in endless forms, then a doctor arrives.

'Hello there, Mum, Dad, and, of course, soldier Louis. I'd like to familiarise you with a trial we would like Louis to take part in. What happens is the computer randomly decides on Louis' particular regime of chemotherapy. I'll leave you with some information [a large red file full of incomprehensible rubrics] . . . In a nutshell, it's called *randomisation*. The patient will receive four courses of chemotherapy, each consisting of a different cocktail of drugs, chosen randomly by a computer. And if you could decide by the morning, please.' He stops speaking.

I can't stop obsessing over the word randomisation. Random. Do I put my son's health in the hands of a computer? I discuss this with my husband while changing baby on the bed. She seems to know not to cry; she's the only child in there with hair.

We have to decide by morning, but I can't read the red file. I would ask God or the Universe, but I've stopped believing in anything. This is a war zone. We decide to go ahead with the trial. I go home to be with the girls. One night on, one night off is our pattern. I try to be a normal mum, but I panic when I leave him, terrified that that he will die when I'm not there. I have trouble sleeping. India has the hardest job: being in the real world, still at school, fielding difficult questions about whether her brother is going to live.

There is a parents' room in the hospital with a chair and a box of tissues. I cry in there. I can't stop, I scare myself. I smoke a roll-up on the street outside. Before Louis' first general anaesthetic (the first of six to give him a lumbar puncture and to put in a Hickman line) I impress on the nurses how I MUST be there when he comes around. I want to be the first person he sees, but Louis is wheeled back to the bay awake. I'm furious.

'Why didn't you tell me where to wait so I could be with him? When he wakes up? Me? His mother?' I am beside myself. I quickly learn which battles to fight in the hospital. This is not one of them, but I feel hugely upset.

*

The first bag of chemo is hooked up to his Hickman line just above his heart and slowly infused into his blood over three days, and as the chemo drips in my son's spirit seems to drip out.

Nothing happens for three days, and for three weeks Louis suffers high temperatures, chest infections, constipation that makes him cry, pustular rashes all over his legs, nausea. He has the first of thirty-five blood transfusions. He becomes thin and weak with no appetite. He loses his joy. He smells different.

One day he asks, 'Mum? Have I got cancer?'

I put crystals under his pillow and move my hands over his sleeping body. I pray on my knees. 'Yes, God, I'm sorry about earlier. I'll do anything.'

Louis says, 'My heart hurts in my sleep.'

He dreams of pain.

I don't know what to do with my fear and grief and trauma in the face of seeing my son suffer. Of the fact he may die. It is literally one breath at a time, a lot of tears and an absolute rule that when I'm on the ward, I'm strong. For him, for all the children, the nurses and the parents. It takes every ounce of strength. I can cry when I leave.

My father visits. He too has cancer, and his face is puffed up by steroids. He sits Louis on his knees in the parents' room. Big bear, little bear. He tries to make Louis laugh, though that is getting harder. Ella (aged one) with her long curls and little nurse's outfit punctures the sadness, brings welcome smiles. She totters around, pulling open hospital curtains in other bays saying, 'Hello, darling!' to whoever is inside.

Nurse

Right, new mum. I've cleared a cupboard for you. You must label all your personals. Now, if you could try and get Louis to eat a tiny bit of toast today that would be great.

It's not a kitchen. It's a stainless-steel coffin. It's about two feet between each counter, meaning that only two parents at a time can be in there. A woman enters the kitchen, stressed, angry.

Angry Mum Melanie

Excuse me. Sorry, just let me move my vegetables. You've just arrived? Ah. Where's my sharp knife? I do wish people wouldn't use my special sharp knife because now it isn't going to be sharp . . . or special . . . I've been here before, you know. I did it all two years ago. He's only gone and bloody relapsed. So, here we go again. This hospital has killed us. Killed the family. All this treatment. It's unending. Anyway, welcome to the madhouse. Excuse me, here I go again. Another meal wasted.

As Louis' leukaemia is so aggressive we will probably be in hospital solidly for four to six months. I had been about to travel to Edinburgh to star in the all-female sitcom, my double act with Michelle Gomez, which we had co-created. I was in denial and wanted them to postpone, but it's been recast. They can't wait for me. I didn't realise then that I would not be working for nearly two years.

We have no money. One of us needs to be at home, with Ella and India, or at hospital, with Louis, at all times, so we simply cannot earn a living. The mortgage company are sympathetic but won't give us a mortgage holiday. People reach out with charitable foundations to contact: the Actors' Charitable Trust, the Ralph Richardson Foundation. I write a begging letter of sorts, laying out our predicament: neither of us can work, we need to care for Louis round the clock, and we have a small child and another in primary. I send the letter to everyone in my address book and then I ask my mum for all her friends' addresses. I explain that we need to have help covering our costs for a year and then we will put the remaining money into building a much needed garden on site at the hospital. The money starts to come in and the donations make me cry. Especially the anonymous ones, where there's no need for thanks or even a text: 'Just go ahead. Cover your costs for three months. I'm here for you.' Friends continued to operate a rota, making sure there was food every night for our hospital return, sending hampers or banned goodies to Louis in the hospital, cleaning the house, building the fire, feeding the cat, texting daily messages of hope.

I learned a lot about giving in those two years. I've learned never to say, 'If there's anything I can do,' because there always is.

I started experiencing what I now know were panic attacks during nights I was not at the hospital. I breathed through it, but I longed to be hugged and held. My husband and I seemed unable to console each other; we were both locked in fear and grief. We passed like ships in the night, passing the baby over, incanting again and again, 'We are here for Louis. He comes first.' But we were beginning to fall apart. (I later read that over eight per cent of relationships fail in these sorts of stressful, dire situations.)

Louis has another general anaesthetic and a lumbar puncture. Chemo is infused over four days, and then four weeks of illness follow. A frightening allergic reaction to the platelets in a supercharged bag of blood. Suddenly, the bay is full of doctors and nurses. He has turned beetroot red and is smacking his face and crying. I am crying. It takes an hour to calm him and control the rash. It's the most awful hour. Could he die? I feel completely helpless. I have no way of knowing how to cope with the constant fear of his death. There isn't a handbook or manual for this. I just stay as close to him as possible, and then have a panic attack when I go home to the girls in case he dies while I am not there.

Louis is very thin. He gets his head shaved. He keeps finding his eyelashes in his tea. I dream of a dead dog washed up on the tide. We both cry a lot and we decide crying's okay.

I sleep in a bed like a tiny matchbox next to him, animal-patterned curtains strobing in front of our eyes. Nurses swish in and out fifty times a day. They can't knock, obviously, so they come in when you're naked, crying, stroking your son's head, rowing with your husband. I keep Louis' hair in a yellow plastic hospital bag. When I first saw all the bald kids, I thought they looked awful. They look more and more beautiful every day.

Deranged. Out of range. Unanchored. All at sea. The dictionary calls deranged 'insane'. All I could focus on was keeping Louis alive, waking all through the night when his machines began beeping, monitoring his temperature, trying to keep his spirits up. It was deepest winter, but on every hospital day I would throw myself at dawn into Tooting Lido to be able to cope with the day and night on that ward. The shock of the cold helped to numb the endless sense of dread in the pit of my stomach and allowed me to make sure I was my best when I buzzed in to the hospital ward. No tears – only positivity and puppet shows.

The PTSD only hits after the event. At the time, I was one hundred per cent focused in the ward but when I got home at night I would collapse into crashes of uncontrollable tears. When Louis was finally asleep at night, I would roll a joint and smoke it outside in the children's play area, in the Wendy house. It was medication of sorts, because I didn't dare start on any antidepressants, even though they were offered. The steady stream of requests quickly became overwhelming.

No, to the counsellor.

No, to the chaplain.

No, to the pills.

Please, please, just leave us be.

A nurse bustles in to review Louis' pain chart, so that we can all get to grips with his pain relief. We encourage Louis to point to the face that describes him best – ranging from bright smiles ('no pain') through to deepest anguish ('hurts badly'). My heart breaks when he points to 'hurts badly'.

After a few months, my agent gets in touch with a voice-over job, and I accept that financially I have to take it. The hours would be short, and I hoped I could finish quickly to return to the hospital. It felt surreal to have to return to work, to a sense of regular, normal life. Every moment I am away from Louis, I obsess. I think I will be all right to get through the first day, but after the recording is done I am sick in the toilet. It was too much.

Ad Agency Girl

Hi, Doon! So brave of you to do this for us. Are you coping? Just tell me everything. I can take it. (*She wells up*)

Is he going to . . . make it? Don't give him chemo. It's positively medieval . . . Right! Let's go. I expect you've got to get back to the hospital, bless you. I've got four children and, touch wood, they're all okay . . . So, can we have it light and sexy with a bit of a smile in the voice? Okay?

As the weeks tick past, a sort of Tourette's-type swearing begins to consume my everyday activities. If a match won't light, it's a 'twatting shitbox of a fuck match', a car going a wee bit slowly in front of me is 'a fucking lump of gold shit'. My rage is boundless. I escape the hospital sometimes to Banstead High Street, the local village, and find I'm sobbing in a café called Edibles while two old ladies stare at me. I get recognised looking vacantly at nylon blouses in a second-hand shop I shouldn't even be in, my eyes puffy as infected footballs.

I become an expert in efficient crying in mundane places:

1) Driving in the car (loud and guttural and free);
2) Hospital car park before heading back in (snivelling, choking);
3) In the swimming pool (miming front crawl, bawling when taking a breath);
4) Eating and drinking (trying to do both, swallow and cry);
5) Alone at home (the stoic single tear).

I use the disabled badge issued to us when in a rush to buy Louis a dish he might actually eat from the local Waitrose, but incur the wrath of the old people of Banstead, frowning at me as I park, so I limp spectacularly and look at their sheepish faces. I hate them. How I hate them. I hate them inside the supermarket even more when they tut behind me in the queue because I have inevitably forgotten my purse and so am scrabbling and babbling into my bag trying to scrape enough change together. And, yes, I'm sure they tut again, the old of Banstead, so I move aside with a flourish.

'Please, please, go ahead. I'm so sorry I'm wasting your time that would obviously be better spent eating biscuits in a church hall. Please, please, go ahead. I must have left my purse IN THE CHILDREN'S CANCER WARD UP THE ROAD WHERE MY TEN-YEAR-OLD SON IS SUFFERING FROM ACUTE MYLOID LEUKAEMIA. Be my guest!'

I am escorted from the premises by a large security guard from Newcastle. I'm informed that I'm barred. Barred from Waitrose in Banstead.

As Louis' randomised trial progresses, he is given a new drug called MACE. It's delivered by a chatty man in a hazard suit. It's bright blue, like Jeyes toilet cleaner, and is slowly infused into Louis' Hickman line. The computer decides that this is his last round. If this fails, it is a bone marrow transplant.

Another six weeks of terrible illnesses pass in a blur, before the final session is upon us. Louis is given a general anaesthetic and lumbar puncture. After an anxious wait, we are finally told that there were no blast cells found. He is officially in remission. I whoop on Clapham High Street and tell perfect strangers that my son is in remission. He will be an outpatient until he is eighteen, and every time we leave the hospital we head-bang to Led Zeppelin all the way home.

Thirteen

The Primadoona

After great pain, a formal feeling comes –
The Nerves sit ceremonious, like Tombs –
The stiff Heart questions 'was it He, that bore,'
And 'Yesterday, or Centuries before'?

The Feet, mechanical, go round –
A Wooden way
Of Ground, or Air, or Ought –
Regardless grown,
A Quartz contentment, like a stone –

This is the Hour of Lead –
Remembered, if outlived,
As Freezing persons, recollect the Snow –
First – Chill – then Stupor – then the letting go –

Emily Dickinson, 'After Great Pain'

When Louis came home he was painfully thin, bald and pale, with his nose tube taped to his face. Kids would stare when we walked down the street, and I would stride ahead to shield him and purposefully command more attention so that he could walk undisturbed. He slept in our bed where his night feeding through a tube could be monitored by me and my husband. If I increased the feed in an attempt to get him to gain weight, he'd wake up in the morning feeling horribly sick and angry with me. But he had little appetite, and I was worried to see him so frail.

We attempted, as we had at the Marsden, to do some schoolwork on the bed. Somehow it all felt meaningless, learning about the First World War, fractions. He wasn't well enough to go to school so this was a strange purgatory: out of hospital but still bed-ridden and weak. His bravery and dignity was astounding, humbling. He just got through it. Meanwhile, I was rebuilding the shattered fragments of my family.

Eventually, he crept to a semblance of health. He had many, many illnesses along the road – too many nights spent taking him to hospital at 3 a.m. for antibiotics. The dead days, trying to keep his spirits up, driving around Camberwell, smoking out the window. Never quite out of the woods. His hair came back curly, and he went back to school for the final three months of primary school. Back home it was hard to adjust after the initial euphoria. I had a sort of ghastly superiority with other people, a kind of red card I kept in my pocket that I could always whip out to trump their pain, their stupid obsessions, loft conversions, bad haircuts, arguments, minor skin complaints . . . yes, yes, poor you, but has your ten-year-old son just come out of a cancer ward? Lucky to be alive? Red card!

I wanted people to really understand what Louis had been through, so one night, incensed by watching a preening, smug comedian on TV, I sat down at the kitchen table and started writing Louis' story as a script. I contacted the hospital, asking if it would be possible to have his notes. They declined, as parents sometimes use these notes to try to sue the hospital if their children die. They want to know if the hospital has done everything they could have, which is tragic but understandable. But I had got to know many of the staff – the ward matron, the indomitable nurses and the admin team – after the creation of a respite garden in the hospital grounds with a donation from our generous donors. So, I went in for a meeting and explained my predicament, letting them know that, if anything, it was a huge work of praise for the team that nursed Louis. They relented. I got a huge stack of Louis' notes, which took days and a river of tears to wade through. Every medication administered, every bad reaction, temperature, stool consistency – you name it. The notes were exhaustive, but gold dust for me.

I soon realised no one wanted this amount of detail. The show needed to show him, his bravery, the children around him, the nurses, the parents, the siblings. I made a start and wrote when I could. Once it was finished, I sent a small excerpt to a favourite director, Simon Godwin, at the Royal Court and asked him to direct. Mercifully, he said yes. I wanted it to be funny, revealing, truthful, dreadful: everything we had endured distilled into an hour's script. I had been offered the Gilded Balloon at the Edinburgh Festival for its premiere, a few months away, so Simon and I decided to have a week's workshop.

It didn't work. It was too brutal, too raw, and he found it hard to cut or, indeed, criticise. It was too painful. After three days we decided to cancel Edinburgh and postpone until the following year. It needed a radical rewrite with a professional, so I sent it to Bryony Lavery, a playwright I hugely admired, and she dropped the project she was working on and said yes.

Then the *really* painful work began. We decided that she should have a pass at it, meaning take what was the bare bones and rewrite. After a month I was sent her script. It felt wrong, out of kilter, not authentic and not my voice. Taking it away from the personal, the overly confessional, she had put it in a voice that I just could not get comfortable with. She had upped the comedy but made me a sort of arch actress unhappy with playing the Cancer Mother role. This definitely worked in certain places, but in others it grated horribly.

Did I have to choose? Bryony and I discussed it, and then we rewrote together in her kitchen every day for three weeks, in front of a tiny coal fire. Everything changed, evolved: the tone, the structure. It was painful, but we cracked it. Finally, we had a script we could rehearse.

By this time our lovely director had been asked to join Bristol Old Vic and to take on other high-profile projects. To his very great credit he cleared, to his new boss's great annoyance, three weeks to get this show on its feet. So, a year later, we went back into the same rehearsal room and made a start. Bryony came for the first few days – I felt a huge weight of pressure and nervousness to make it work. It wasn't what it had been previously: it told a story clearly, so everyone would see what a journey this small boy had been on. Whole pieces that I thought were absolute gold dust were binned, other delights discovered; there were cuts, additions, rewrites. After three weeks Simon and Bryony thought I should do a reading in front of a small audience before I finalised the script. Just to feel and gauge audience feedback. I read it and leapt about a bit in a tiny sixty-seater in St James's with some invited friends. I don't think I have ever felt so nervous. No music, basic lighting, no props – but its essence was there and it worked and people were laughing and crying. We reworked again and I went to Edinburgh.

That August I performed *Primadoona* forty times in the Dining Room of the Gilded Balloon, a dark box of a theatre with an unbroken rake of a hundred and fifty seats. I had to get changed in a sort of corridor with four or five other productions rushing in and out. The most basic props were laid out on our very bare stage: a pair of red wellington boots, a Man United pillow case, a flamenco dress, a hospital screen and an old-fashioned phone, spotlit on a plinth. My pre-show music came on. I stood in the shadows underneath the audience, feeling sick and excited, and we were off.

I remember thinking about ten minutes in, 'God, it's still me talking!'

It was so hard not to judge myself while I was still performing; there were so many characters to play. Exhausting monologues full of medications, a couple of high-energy clown routines. Again, people laughed. People cried.

Louis came to see it a couple of times and joined me for the curtain call. My son, who was by some miracle alive. As they say, 'not a dry eye in the house'. I won a Fringe First and the show got a run at the Menier Chocolate Factory, but the best award in the world was my son's continuing health.

There has to be a decent amount of time, I think, between trauma and the writing of it, and the show after all its cancellations, rewrites and reworkings packed a powerful punch. As Melissa Febos says, 'expressive writing about trauma strengthens the immune system, decreases obsessive thinking and contributes to the overall health of the writer'.

When people make art of out pain the response can be 'Ooh, I bet that was cathartic'. Cathartic? A little bit more than that, I think. There was something so visceral about the show that people really responded to, and led to frequent requests to restage it, but it was definitely of the moment. It was healing for me to perform, and for the audience, and Louis, to see. Now, there is simply the infinite daily gratitude that he is alive, and that feeling never goes.

Making sense of pain. Isn't that what trying to lead a happy life is?

Fourteen

The German Air Hostess

Casting Call
Heavyweight comedy actress required for
farce in the West End to play Gretchen,
a larger-than-life, passionate, histri-
onic German air hostess. Expert at
physical comedy with laser-like timing,
she is loud, highly strung and vaguely
ridiculous. She is ebullient, exhausting
and deeply romantic.

As Louis limped back to health at home, my dear father Rocky passed away after a long battle with prostate cancer. He had visited Louis in hospital many times when both of them were very ill (big bear, little bear), sitting with Louis on his knee, both with cancer – how did this happen? My husband had lost his father to cancer just before we were admitted to hospital, so they became the bookend grandfathers. But when did we have time to grieve, now that our son was home? He needed full-time care, he still had a nose tube for feeding, nurses came every second day, and we had many hospital visits. My grief was put on hold, but I had lost a vital rock in my life and felt just a little bit more unstable. The money we had so generously been given was gone, half into a garden that was built into the Marsden just after we left, and we were beginning to sink into debt. I suppose I didn't yet know the ravages of post-traumatic stress on the body or the mind. There was simply no time to heal or process. We needed the money. I didn't have counselling, I didn't have time.

I was offered a part in a West End play called *Boeing-Boeing*. It was a four-month commitment, and I just couldn't see any other way around it. It was an expertly crafted farce centred round a Lothario who has Italian, English and German fiancées, each a beautiful air hostess, unaware of the others' existence. As one air hostess leaves, another arrives for her particular 'lay-over'. He manages to keep one up, one down and one pending until, due to unexpected schedule changes, they all arrive at his house in Paris at the same time. Confusion! Accents! Slapstick routines! The wages would dig us out of a hole, and I said yes, despite the fact that deep cracks were opening up in our marriage and were widening. We were broken, going through the motions. I just wanted the kids to be able to live normal lives, with us all at home, and to try and stop the marriage from collapsing.

In no way did I feel ready. I was exhausted, stressed, stick-thin, smoking, afraid all the time that Louis would relapse, afraid that the girls had been irreparably damaged, afraid that my marriage was in meltdown. Not a great recipe for a West End farce, but I had no time to process. It was eight shows a week and no understudies. The show must go on.

By the time of the opening night I felt under-rehearsed, terrified and spectacularly unfunny. I hated rehearsals, which were normally my favourite bit, but I suppose I was just constantly averting a sort of nervous collapse. I mastered a German accent and I cried a lot. Luckily, the maid in the show was Rhea Perlman, a comedy heroine of mine, and in rehearsals she laughed like a drain at pretty much anything I did, which was the tonic I needed to actually get me on stage. Backstage each night, loathing the thought of going on, trying to psych myself up, I would dedicate the show to one child I had known at the hospital who had died. Sadly, there were seven. That was my ritual to get me through, to remember those children.

At the end of each show I would come home, and my husband and I would sit at opposite ends of the sofa in stony silence. We had vowed at the beginning, at Louis' diagnosis, that we would fight for him and our family above all else. It was inconceivable that we would part – after all we had been through, we just had to work harder. How could we do that to the children? But we became two hardened stones, barely functioning, going through the motions, getting up in the night for a teething child, shopping, attempting to eat. The iceberg was getting closer, but neither of us had the strength to change course.

We spectacularly hit the ice one afternoon, halfway through the run of *Boeing-Boeing*. It was not dignified. I am far from proud of it, but it happened and it was the end. I moved out for a while, but it was clear this wasn't going to mend.

I was performing Gretchen, eight shows a week, barely eating. Rhea kept me going. She was my saviour. During those very worst of weeks I couldn't stop sobbing. She would come into my dressing room, brisk, New York, no-nonsense. 'Okay, Doonie, let's go, let's go, get your shoes on . . .' She got me on the stage countless times, but my level of exhaustion was dangerous, my eyes puffy as infected golfballs. I was running on empty. At one point in the show I had to throw myself to the floor in a paroxysm of love and exclaim, 'But I luff him so maatch!'

And then sob. The audience adored it. The better I did it, the longer the laugh and applause, and the longer I could lie on the floor and rest. I didn't want to get up. I could hardly stand. I regularly cried all the way home in taxis and sometimes, God bless them, they would waive the fare, which would make me cry more.

The run ended, and very sadly, we divorced. The house went on the market and I really started to unravel.

What does it mean to break down? Is it like Ruby Wax suddenly finding herself crawling on her hands and knees on the playing field at the school sports day? Having 'a little rest' in a psychiatric unit dosed up on a cocktail of drugs? Being zapped like women of my mother's generation with electricity for being 'hysterical and unstable'?

Looking back, I think during this period, and up to two years later, I had a series of mini-breakdowns – like tiny explosions that caused maximum damage. I was barely functioning. A friend had given me 'a care package' of drugs to get me through. Sleeping pills, Xanax and who knows what else. They stayed in my desk, and even when I experienced my first panic attack, I didn't touch them. This made me feel strong. I was afraid of my need for oblivion. Addiction runs strongly in my family, and I was afraid of falling into its grip. The sudden swooping night of a sleeping pill. The groggy dead feeling in the morning.

The house went on the market, and I kept it maniacally tidy, sitting in the garden in the twilight with Ella and India while various young couples looked around. A few months after the split, Louis and I had a terrible row and I banished him to his dad's. Although I try to have no regrets and think I was doing my best, I do regret this. That day was so painful, and he stayed with his father for weeks. My heart broke. I took a Xanax, but it didn't work. You cannot bury grief. It will rise. It will seek you out.

I felt a terrible debilitating guilt at splitting the family up. We would meet at a local pizza place on

Sundays to try and have 'a family lunch'. Ella used to try and make my soon-to-be-ex and me hold hands. It was deeply painful.

Louis stayed mostly at his father's, so his room, replete with football shirts and drum kits became something of a museum, or a shrine. India took the opportunity to go wild, and the neighbours constantly complained, even calling the police when her friends climbed onto the roof, played music through the night, smoked weed in the garden.

So, it was my little girl and I trailing around the common on a Sunday, me obsessed with swans because they mate for life, pole-axed by grief. I was very hard on myself. I felt like a failure in every department.

That Christmas, I took the family to Goa. After holding on to all that tension I let go a little. I constantly cried and felt scared for my mental health. I was irritable, then elated. I smoked roll-ups, I shouted. I'll never forget one day on the vast Goan beach, listening to 'Mr. Brightside' by The Killers on my daughter's headphones with my kids all around me. The sudden, glorious, flooding sound of that song, of anarchy and rage and sex and jealousy. I started dancing. At first to make the kids laugh like I used to, like I hadn't done for months, maybe years. I ran around them like a mad bird, head-banging, high-kicking, grinding, twerking, maniacal, free. I was hysterical. I was coming out of my cage, my prison, the hospital, the pent-up tears, the pain, the guilt, the torment, the sword of Damocles always hanging just above my head, always waiting, expecting bad things to happen. I twisted, I shrieked, I cried with laughter as the kids doubled up and the beach-dwellers looked panicked and then a bit disgusted. I twirled like a possessed fiend, like a fury. I suddenly was free. Louis was alive. I could still dance. I felt *joy*, swift, painful, liberating. I collapsed on the sand. There will never be a dance like it. I could never recreate it because it was so close to real desperation and collapse, because I was hanging on by a thread. But I had, at last, remembered how to laugh. My children and my best friend were watching. We had survived, but the battle scars were deep – though they say those heal even more strongly, like a stronger skin. It would be a long road for me to feel balanced, joyful and free again.

Fifteen

The Alcoholic Single Actress

Casting Call
Frances is a forty-something, sexually adventurous, childless actress, single best friend of the lead protagonist. She is horrified by roles offered to her in later life — 'ageing German prostitute' and 'lonely spinsters'. She is sassy and charismatic and starting to drink too much so a whiff of desperation is creeping in around the edges.

After selling the family home, my ex and I were doomed to separate rentals. A few days after moving into my new flat, we were burgled and the car was stolen. Luckily, the kids were all at my ex's and I had been out with my brother till late. I was most upset at the loss of the super-woofers in the back of my Volvo and my epic CD collection. Damn them in the getaway car, speeding off to Sly and the Family Stone. Que será, será.

As we rolled into the next home, all our worldly belongings were piled onto the communal forecourt of our new mansion block: stained sofas, rugs full of wax and red wine, mattresses of blood-spotted embarrassments, many more tropical plants than furniture, and hundreds of pictures. I began to feel like the gypsy mother, moving on, downsizing, dragging the kids into all our different new homes. I was a single parent, and there was literally no alternative. People often ask me why I've moved so much, and the answer is money. This business is feast or famine. The guilt has to take second place to the food on the table. I remember that day – Louis and India came to help me move with mates from college, and I felt a surge of hope. Perhaps we could all live here together in peace, put the past behind us.

The communal gardens by my new flat were beautiful, two acres presided over by a two-hundred-year-old mulberry tree. Little did I know that in the ensuing years I would move another five times, always due to financial or school circumstances. I was a single mother now with a rescue Staffy pup named Rocky and three children who basically l ived with me. I had to earn. There was no maintenance. We had done a clean break, split the money – no lawyers for us – so the stresses were high.

It turned out, at first happily, that Louis wanted to be with us all, so we set up his bed in half of the sitting room. But we were heading down a dark road. The woman in the flat above hated us. There was always the smell of smoke or weed as soon as I entered the front door. Louis and India brought friends round and congregated in the communal areas. Eventually, there were emails to all the residents. Reports of 'suspicious people' at my door. Louis and India were at the local academy; these were their friends. But I began to lose control of them and myself, Ella still being at primary and me trying to protect her. I was the lone she-wolf, the gypsy, smoking silently on the swing seat in the dark, unable to control her teens or her tears, menopausal, half-mad.

We were all in post-traumatic stress after Louis and the cancer-ward years, and that brought on an early menopause. I felt deranged and unable to cope. My mood swings become more intense. I cried a lot, sweated a lot, shouted a lot, tried to be normal, to tag the kids if they were out very late, never knowing quite where they were. No rules followed, phones turned off, coming in at 3 a.m., waking Ella, more rows. Hell. I was deranged with anger when I heard the word 'bitch' in gangsta rap coming from bedrooms. I would bang on the doors and start shouting, demanding they turn it off.

One Sunday morning, the Xbox console was booming from the sitting room. There were take-away cartons and empty cans of Tango everywhere. Shooting, shooting, then shouting. I walked in to find Louis and three of his friends. No one looked up. I was invisible to them despite being severely ill with bronchitis.

'Could you clear the rubbish and turn it down, please?'

Nothing. Not one glance up from the game. I felt rage. I picked up the Xbox, took it out to the hall and smashed it on the doorstep. I kicked the boys out and I kicked Louis out to his dad's. This became the pattern for the next three years. I was at breaking point.

A particular low was being taken to the garden by the children, India and Louis, so that they could have a talk with me. I was in a shabby grey dressing gown with a murky fleecy collar and a deep rattling cough.

'We think you should be on medication. You're out of control. It's like you're mad.'

There was a flash of empathy across my son's face as he saw me about to cry, then swallow tears and be stoic. Medication? Maybe I needed it. Sleeping pills. Antidepressants. That was a rock-bottom moment, as I coughed and sweated into another sleepless night alone, trying to be a happy mum. Failing. The processing of pain and trauma is a long road. There's no quick fix. Pills may do it for a while, or weed, drugs, drink, sex, but the damage is there and must be addressed, or it will haunt you.

This was the point where seeking help was essential, but my self-care was at the bottom of the to-do list, financially and emotionally. I was afraid of my state of mind, my mood swings and my anxiety. Sudden shouting, then sudden calm. Where was this heading? I was exhausted and thin, and trying to do craft with my six-year-old while sending texts to my older kids, trying to mask my worry when I didn't know where they were. I felt old, isolated and full of grief. I was operating in the dark.

Around this time, Ella had a friend sleep over one evening. They'd just done a long, very long, puppet show for me, and I had got them to bed. A knock on the door. It was a policeman. My son Louis was in hospital. Could I come now?

'Was he injured?' I asked.

'Yes'.

'How did it happen?'

He said we'd talk on the way. I was like a wild animal, needing to get to him. I ran and knocked next door, and the husband answered. Could he come and wait at mine for the two little girls until I returned home from the hospital? He had two boys and a wife in a wheelchair. I literally had no other option. He came over and sat with the girls.

I left with the policeman and texted India. She replied and arranged to meet me at the hospital. He was at King's A&E department. King's, the same hospital where he'd been in and out for a year after cancer treatment with all the illnesses he had suffered at the tail end of chemo. Questions asked in the police car, shaking, feeling like I was going to be sick. He was found on the pavement, unconscious, by a fire crew who were working on a house opposite. His clothes had been cut off him in case of stab wounds. When I got to him, he was in boxers with his head taped into a large square frame, retching into a cardboard bowl, his clothes in a plastic bag at his bedside. More and more of his friends arrived, outraged. He'd been walking down the street to his dad's new house, about 7 p.m., summer, light. Three men, one older, two younger, started hassling him. They threatened him for being in 'the wrong postcode', and the upshot was that he was kicked unconscious and left on the roadside. He could so easily have been killed. My son. Who nearly died, then nearly died again.

The rage I felt began gathering like a dangerous twister on the horizon. I was so, so angry. Here he was in hospital after beating death once with cancer. But then I caught myself. The thought of all the boys killed on our streets. The mothers. The families. The pain. Yes, I'm angry, but he's alive. He's alive.

I spend the next month driving those streets looking for those boy men, those cowards. I look every day. And yes, I feel hatred, anger. What will I do if I see them? Endless, imagined scenarios, like OCD, spitting in their faces, trying to shock them, trying to scare them.

He stays off school for a week. He's beginning to be paranoid about leaving the house and he doesn't feel safe. He begins to always travel with a friend. He becomes reclusive, stuck in his room, not working – sometimes in a room full of boys all vowing to hurt his attackers if they find them. The gangsta rap, the talk of vengeance. The cycle just never ends. Eventually, he recovers. He makes it to Sheffield University, and his life changes for the better.

After he leaves for uni, I audition at the Royal Court for April De Angelis' play *Jumpy*, directed by Nina Raine. The part was a desperate, increasingly alcoholic actress performing outrageous and inappropriate burlesque dances in cottages in Norfolk and being the best friend to the main protagonist, played by Tamsin Greig.

The play centred around a mother's relationship with her errant, rebellious fifteen-year-old daughter. Tamsin had access to a wealth of experience of the real thing in me, as my life was mirroring the art of this play, and she would squeeze every last detail of the latest saga in my life. The show was a hit, and there was talk of transferring later in the year to the West End. Theatre wages do not cut the mustard, particularly for a sole breadwinner, so I took my first in-vision advert, due to my financial situation. The ad was semi-improvised and featured the brilliant Darren Boyd. It was a week's shoot, and I would film the advert in the day and get a courier bike back to the Court to perform at night.

My health was deteriorating, both physically and mentally. I was battling a chest infection, but I just kept pushing on, unable to turn the ad money down. I was working with a temperature, still in denial about the fact that I was making myself seriously ill. On the bike journey to the theatre I would just open the visor of the helmet for the welcome cold air and then perform in the evening after a scalding hot shower as I had chills and the shakes. It was a very lonely time, and I feel both shocked and saddened that I put myself through such dire circumstances while my life was falling apart at the seams. It was a terrible time.

I started taking my third round of high-strength antibiotics. Looking back now, I can clearly recognise the warning signs. I should have pulled out of the show, but with only two weeks to go and all the important people 'in the business' due to come with my agent in the last week, I foolishly soldiered on. I was running on empty, but my body was still moving. It was like a story I'd heard about a woman in the Channel who had died, but her arms were still swimming. A profound exhaustion overcame me before and after the shows. I could barely move, but, on stage, a shot of adrenaline somehow got me through those two weeks.

A few days after the end of the run, I land in hospital with a very serious pneumonia. On the morning I go to A&E, I get a cab with India to the hospital. I wear a black puffer coat, but my face is beetroot red. I'm boiling and freezing and have the most epic migraine building behind my eyeballs. I'm shaking and crying, feeling scared at having lost control of my body. I feel helpless and desperate. I am convinced I am going to die. I have never felt so ill. At the hospital it is hours before I see a doctor. They are filming *24 Hours in A&E* in the waiting room, and I lie on the floor and sob while India keeps the cameras away. Finally, I get an X-ray.

The doctor declares it is a 'crackling pneumonia' and points to a large, dark patch at the centre of my chest. I try to ignore the excitement in his voice and peer at the image, even though my vision is blurred. The headache is now beyond description, and I can barely breathe. Crackling, shallow breath and the shakes, I'm more like an old woman than someone who has recently been performing eight shows a week at the Royal Court. I'm trolleyed up to the respiratory ward and walk, unsteady on my feet, into a tiny, coffin-like room with a commode. One chair, one window high up like a monastery. I am certain this is where it's all going to end.

They put a canula in and a shitload of intravenous antibiotics, but initially they can't pinpoint exactly why I am so ill. I am allergic to some of the antibiotics and come out in a raised red rash all over my body. I piss all over the floor when squatting over the commode. I have a ridiculous nightie, flapping open at the back. I take the shallowest of breaths and wash in and out of consciousness. Even when I try to breathe deeply, the tiniest amount goes in. It's all crackle and wheeze. I start to panic, feeling like I can't breathe.

Friends come and lay a tablecloth on my body, spoon soup in my mouth. After ten minutes I'm exhausted. I have lost so much weight I'm like a head in a bed. Different consultants enter, looking puzzled. I'm in there for seven days, with hazy memories of brusque nurses changing cannulas, painful flushing of the tubes, new antibiotics, a livid red rash all over my body.

On my final day I am taken for a brutal bronchoscopy – the closest thing I can imagine to medieval torture – where two nurses hold me down as they spray stinging anaesthetic into my nose and put a camera into my lungs. It is terrifying to feel so powerless. I feel particularly lonely with no 'significant other' to be there at the end of this nightmare.

I have my 'angel' (my best friend Sharon), many close and wonderful friends and family, but I have rarely felt so 'single', so in need of being reassured, of being held. It wasn't exactly self-pity, but a terrible sense of death and being on my own. I get to go home eventually and slowly recuperate. Mum, sister, friends, all looking after Ella and feeding me.

I recover. I take longer walks, like an old lady on the common. I feel like it was a big lesson burned into me. Why did I push myself almost to death's door? Why, as women, is it so hard to say no, to pull out, to let people down, to actually ask for help? For me, it was financial worries, needing to do the advert to pay the rent as theatre work wasn't covering it. Perhaps it was also fear of the future, of no work if I pulled out of the run, of letting everyone down. I had a long time to think about this as I recuperated. I ate, I rested, I let others take the weight, I slowly got well – and I learned to say no. Pain, rage, despair, death, leukaemia and divorce. Yep, something had to give!

Sixteen

The Desperate Cougar

Casting Call
A good-looking actress in her early forties, required to play guest lead in a hit Channel 4 sitcom. She comes on to a much younger man and tries to snare him in her web. A classic cougar, still hot, despite her age. Highly sexed, fruity and single. You can tell she was a catch in her day. A man-eater.

During the run of *Jumpy*, I auditioned for a popular TV comedy guest lead. The part was a rather desperate cougar trying to get off with the younger man: she is sexually voracious, desperate and ridiculous. (Of course, the part was written by a man.) It's a hit show on Channel 4, and I flick

169

through the script, angered by the tone of the part, but the director is someone I've worked with on a BBC sitcom, so I think together we will find an interesting way to do it. He'd been to my house for dinner. We got on. I liked his wife. I was looking forward to catching up.

I wait in the freezing cold church on a bright autumn morning, eyeing the other actresses who are also waiting outside. By this point I've recovered from pneumonia and am actually performing *Jumpy* in the West End, recuperated, paid well and back on my feet. Herbs, yoga, meditation, healing. I was back.

A snippy little casting agent jerks his head at me to summon me into the room, indicating that it's my turn. I'm furious already.

Snippy Casting Agent
Oh, I saw *Jumpy*.

Doon
Oh, great.

(*The silence is deafening. You complete ****, I think.*)

I see the director. I open my arms to give him the 'Wow! It's been such a long time' hug, but he's playing the director power game. He's playing it cool. He indicates a low sofa opposite and, yes, horror of horror, there is a girl filming the audition from the back corner.

Doon
Wow! So, you're still living in Chiswick?

Director
No, I live in a big house in Lyme Regis.
(*Did he actually say that?*)

Doon
Well, good. Good for you. I've moved too.

Director
So, Doon, what did you think of the part?

Doon
Well, I'm interested in finding a different way of playing the desperate cougar. I wondered about subverting it slightly so that she's actually celebrated for her sexuality rather than being a ghastly black widow spider, ensnaring the young boy into her web.

(*He looks disdainful and bored.*)

Director
Well, let's read some, shall we?

The camera is on. I read the part three times, attempting each time through characterisation to expand and subvert this dangerous stereotype. A desperate cougar in search of young blood. The director remains silent, clearly unimpressed and patently not wanting this invention. He likes the stereotype – nothing alternative or challenging. The assistant filming goes very red and squirms on my behalf. She can sense my discomfort. Yet again, as from the early days as a stereotyped 'feed', I am being asked to play a very small part of what I could contribute. Sticking me behind a desk, asking me to be strict, to be sexual, to not illustrate the story with my body, is a repression. As the director idly flicks through the script, clearly bored, I suddenly get up and announce that I have to leave.

Doon
Sorry, but I'm gonna have to go now.

My bag is sadly upside down as I grab it and a

million things clunk to the floor, rolling hither and thither. I am flustered and grab as much as I can before hotfooting it out of there, red, raging. The fact that I am being filmed only adds to the humiliation. I push open the fire doors as I can't find the actual door and set off all the fire alarms. Weeeeeooooo! Weeeeeooooo! Weeeeeooooo!

An old lady suddenly in hot pursuit.

Old Lady
It was very clear not to push the doors.

I get onto Tottenham Court Road, both my middle fingers aloft. An epiphany. Never again. I call my agent.

Doon
I will never audition for comedy ever again!

And I never have.

So, how are you going to keep working, I hear you ask? How do you call the shots in a business that likes to hold women in place and maintain the default power dynamics? It wasn't going to be easy, but I was determined to try.

Seventeen

The Ball-Breaking Dominatrix

Casting Call

Tough, sexy boss, voracious, strict and still 'hot'. Into everything, nothing fazes her, so a wet dream for boys. Cuts to the quick, sharp-tongued and enjoys verbal humiliation. But this is a comedy so let's keep it clean. She is severe, cold-hearted and imperious.

For an actor who prides herself on her physical ability to master character and create comedy – *Smack the Pony* being a playground where I could explore all aspects of my physicality, from sexually inappropriate yoga teacher to lap-dancing a lamppost

– I have spent a surprising amount of time trapped behind a desk listening to men.

It's a position that is sadly all too familiar: from my early TV days as a feed (playing the role of teacher, receptionist and so on) to *The Day Today* and Collaterlie Sisters at the business desk, to my later role in *Toast of London* as the agent Jane Plough. All these women trapped behind a desk, in vehicles predominantly starring male leads. Sticking me behind a desk and asking me to be strict and not to illustrate the story with my body is almost fetishistic and is also a repression – it's just a small part of the package.

While still recovering from pneumonia I get called in for an audition to play Matt Berry's agent in *Toast of London*. I reiterate my position as a non-reading comedy actress, feeling emboldened by my new resolve. This is a huge 'fuck you all' statement. I'm ready to lose a job rather than succumb to another ghastly power trip. Calls go to and fro. They say I have to read. I decline. They come back and assure me that, really, it's just a chemistry read to see if Matt and I can work together. Great, I reply. I don't have a problem with that, but just to be clear, there should be no camera and also no one else in the room apart from Matt. No producers, casting directors, camera operators, executives, because Matt is the writer and he can decide.

By some miracle they agree. Now I'm really cooking. I walk into that audition, and the room is full of the said caravan of onlookers: producers, execs, casting director, plus a small camera. We say our hellos. Again, there is rather an awkward atmosphere when it comes to the 'read' and, rather wondrously, the caravan troops out of the room to allow Matt and me to improvise, unhindered by onlookers with a freedom to explore the real comedy of the scene. I don't imagine the production team have ever had to do this. It was kind of extraordinary. (When I tell fellow actors what happened in both these auditions they are aghast. They would never have 'the balls' to do it, they say, they always need the part too much.) We all need the parts. But sometimes it's great to reverse the power play.

Matt and I improvised a rough scene, then they all trooped back in, asking how it went. It felt awkward. The team were obviously put out that they'd had to leave the room. Who does she think she is? Again, I was pretty sure I didn't have the part.

I got the part. My epiphany had worked. This rarely happens for actors: we *have to* read or risk losing the job. Now we have to 'self-tape', and only very occasionally do you meet the director for a 'chat' or get offered the part outright. This role also involved me mostly behind a desk, being strict. I was playing someone older, so we experimented with fake, exaggerated facelifts and layers of latex on my neck to make it look like she had had work done. When it came to the screening, I repeatedly shouted out, 'It's not my neck!' to the audience.

A week later, a script arrived for a new TV comedy. My role was a ball-breaking dominatrix, a sort of office bitch, mostly behind a desk. But the script, when not too purple and boysy, was very funny, and it suited me to have a small part in a show while I clawed my way back to health. I vowed that this time, in the audition, I would have the power. I wasn't going to read, be filmed, be humiliated, or talked down to by some ghastly casting agent's assistant crazed on power. I was just going to meet the director and decide if I wanted to do it.

The director was all smiles, all flattery, all charm. Did I like the script? Did I feel it gave me enough scope for humour? Then he asked if I would read a bit. The casting director looked a bit ashen.

Casting Director

Oh no. Umm, Doon has specified . . . I did tell
you that . . . um . . . that she doesn't read . . .
for comedy.

Director

Quite right. With your track record. Your back
catalogue. But as you're here, shall we do a
scene?

Doon (disbelief)

Well, no, because . . . I don't read for comedy.

Director

Really? . . . Come on . . .

Doon

Um . . . no.

Director

Come on . . . Pretty please?

How long can this go on for? I shake his hand
when I leave. It was awkward, for sure, but I felt

empowered and thought for certain I hadn't got the job.

I got the job. This felt groundbreaking. Once again I didn't read, and I got the job. Against all the odds.

I went abroad to shoot the show. The fee allowed me to pay for childcare and . . . to get away. To suddenly be on a flight to an unknown city, to meet a new bunch of actors, to put the ghastly last few months of illness and despair behind me. A new start. We arrived at a sprawling ex-communist, crumbling film studio, patrolled by wild dogs, nestled under an imposing mountain. It is criss-crossed with beautiful walks, streams and unusual cafés selling nettle and garlic soup and shopska salads. There are myriad decaying sets spread out for miles: statues, outbuildings, an old aeroplane from the Sixties, an American high street with shops – it all felt very surreal.

Oh, the deep luxury of a hotel and the banter of a new group of people thrown together! My first time away after the hell of illness and hard work. After that first day, it is the boys' show without question – three boys at the centre of the show, three women on the periphery. I get beautiful, hand-dyed dresses in many colours. My hair is plaited and dressed for hours by make-up ladies who sing folk songs between their cigarettes and tell me I look beautiful. The director tells me I look hot. I hate that word – am I supposed to be flattered that he still deems me sexy? Hot like a porn star or hot like a menopausal fifty-year-old? He looks at me like I should be grateful. I glower but say nothing. There may be trouble ahead, as the old song says. At lunch I sit with the boys. There are a lot of boys. The writers, the director. The director's brother, who is the producer. The crew are mostly young and male, and half or more are local. The other women in the show are not filming at the same time as me, so we only make contact at the hotel. It feels like the old stand-up days. Look at the panel shows. Nothing really changes. Or it does, but incredibly slowly.

A director who is also the writer is never my favourite combination. This director desperately wants to tell me how to say my lines, which is a bad sign. He goes round and round the houses trying to find a way to make me say the lines he has written the way he hears them. If he is a good director, he can 'direct' me to the tone he is looking for, the emotion, the action, the active quality of what I'm trying to do, for example to flatter, to debase, to encourage, to poison.

Sadly, this director doesn't know how to do that. I am trying to expand the reductive stereotype of ball-breaking dominatrix by giving her some light and shade, some vulnerability, some human qualities. Good comedy comes from character, nuance, a flick of the eyes as well as 'funny lines', but, to this director, it is basically as if he owns the character because he has written it. He has an impeccably clear vision of her and I'm not quite playing ball. My refusal to read in the audition seems to have led to him feeling the need to assert his power as the result of a perceived imbalance in my favour, and now he's doing his utmost to address this.

It was not a pleasant dynamic.

I am not what is termed 'a technical actress': I probably have three good takes before I start thinking about it too much and start to get progressively worse. If I become too aware of what I'm stressing in the script or what pauses to leave, it literally kills the creativity for me. There can be no comedy invention or room to breathe. Most of my scenes in *Smack the Pony* were done in one or two takes. We were trusted. We didn't even have endings to sketches. This job, by contrast, was uptight, controlled. I was made to do a minimum of six takes before I was allowed to 'noodle' or just do what I liked at the end. But at the end of six takes, or often more, the invention or magic has evaporated. It was the very worst way to work for me.

One memorable and freezing day, I was being carried by three oiled-up, muscly guards on a freezing wind-tunnel set. In the scene, I am being taken away from the crowds to go to my summer residence. I'm being harangued, and leaflets in favour of voting for their new favourite politician are being thrust in my face. My line was, 'Shoo, shoo. Fuck off!'

It was quite a set-up. Take one I thought went pretty well. The sound and camera engineers both laughed (which is very rare) and gave me the thumbs up. The director had shouted 'cut!' and jogged a few hundred yards from the monitor to give me a note. So, I took the note and did it again. And again. And again. And again. And again. I'd begun to lose all sense of the words.

'Look, just stress the first "shoo", throw away the second, tiny pause, then "fuck off", with the stress on the "fuck" and lose your patience with the "off".'

I was losing patience. The oiled-up men were freezing, and so was I. This was a piss-take, an exercise in control. It was fucking with my head. Eventually I shouted, 'DO NOT TELL ME HOW TO SAY THIS LINE ANY MORE.'

We did maybe three more takes, and then I was summoned to the corner of the set. The director was white with rage. I was made to apologise for undermining him in front of all the extras and the crew. Undermining *him*? I was so thoroughly cold and demoralised I found myself apologising for the sake of peace, if nothing else. After three weeks of swallowing my growing impatience and complete nausea at this way of working, I felt ashamed of myself.

Ah! The chains of patriarchy, as Melissa Febos says. We need to be vigilant in unlearning the patriarchy, for 'the mechanisms of accommodation are very quick to engage; a kind of twilight mode of passivity'. I wouldn't call myself exactly passive, but I felt I had to 'keep the peace' rather than provoke a male director's deep displeasure.

When I returned that evening to the hotel, I met the two other actresses in the bar. They had not been having a great time on the show. They felt patronised, sidelined, ignored, like eye candy, and unable to suggest things – frustratingly stereotyped. They felt it was very much a boys' club, but they weren't doing so many takes (the director was probably telling them how to say the lines). It turned out that neither of them returned after a second series was commissioned. Two other actresses were employed and the plot was rewritten. We sat in the bar for hours, and the two women, both in their mid-twenties, talked about their careers to date. One had done an 'art film' where she had stood naked on a table for fourteen days. No one protected her or handed her a robe between takes; she was then assaulted by the director at the wrap party and people turned a blind eye.

Having always been appalled by the lack of protection for actresses on set, I was at this time considering going into drama schools and giving workshops for young actresses and actors about what they should or shouldn't put up with on set and, indeed, advising them to appraise very carefully scripts that required violence against them (usually rape, in the case of women). This was way before the days of intimacy co-ordinators, and while nudity should aways be carefully considered, there is also the issue of a general pervasive violence against women on screen, for example being pulled down stairs by your hair, smacked, punched, cut, thrown into a van – the list is literally endless. Thankfully, there is now more protection for actors on set, and there are also several different groups who go into mainstream schools to talk about consent.

Talking to the two young actresses who had felt sidelined and patronised on set about their work experiences profoundly saddened and enraged me. We all ended up in tears in that bar, hearing about a rape scene which one of them had had to endure. She had lost her voice, so she couldn't shout 'stop!' while being held down by two men. I suppose the whole package galvanised me to write something: my experiences on set, the actresses' stories, the hotel, men in the lifts with women who are really just girls. The rape scenes the actresses had endured. So, I sat for the next week and wrote a sort of rant-speech entitled 'Enough is Enough'. I focused on rape as a human rights violation, and the fact that it has been defined as a form of torture by the international criminal courts. I would argue that film and television are exacerbating this issue, with increasingly hard-core depictions becoming commonplace. Once you've seen it, you can't unsee it; like abuse, it is insidious, attacking the very core of women's confidence and self-esteem.

After the speech was published in the *New Statesman* it went viral and got me a commission to do a Radio 4 documentary entitled *Body Count Rising*. I was ramping up my activism based on what I was experiencing and the stories I was hearing at work.

Women already feel a shame that cripples them in this culture. Shame that they aren't good enough: good enough lovers, mothers, creators, cooks, workers. Shame about their bodies, their fantasies, their inability to speak up, the legacy they pass to their daughters, their violence, their mental health struggles, their loneliness, their despair. Shame is drummed into us early and is utterly paralysing. Shame stops us engaging, taking part, writing, dancing, singing, expressing ourselves. Shame is deep, and this culture holds our heads down by keeping shame high on the agenda. Our entertainment reflects this. Shame her. Cut her. Rape her. Kill her. Shut her up, silence her, it's what we're watching. It's not good enough. Things must change and soon. It's terrible that things have been allowed to persist as long as they have. I want to leave a legacy of fierce determination for my daughters and all young people, to help create safer working conditions for young actors and actresses that are still coming through.

Eighteen

The Hard-Bitten Detective

Casting Call

Attractive female lead, mid-forties, for this groundbreaking detective series using improvisation rather than set dialogue in the scenes. Hard-hitting storylines involving rape, forensics and some upsetting scenes. Tough as old boots, a bit of a drinker, our lead is a no-nonsense force to be reckoned with.

Oh, how we seem to never tire of the hard-bitten detective! Hurray to the 1970s *Cagney and Lacey* series, where women actually got to be something other than victims, where tables were turned. We saw them being mothers, drinking too much, and of course running around with guns and

189

challenging their chief. But mostly it's a man playing the role of the driven and fiercely determined detective. Even within female-led crime shows such as *Marcella*, *Happy Valley* and *Unforgotten*, the stories hover around serial killers, sexual abusers, stalkers.

I was offered the role of a hard-bitten detective – lots of juicy skeletons in her cupboard, a borderline drink problem and so on – but she was sold to me as a kickass, no-nonsense piece of hardness. This show was different: it was to be improvised, which I found exciting. Maybe I could get out from behind the desk? I took the meeting. But my first question, the million-dollar question:

Doon

How many storylines involve violence against women?

TV Exec

Oooh, let's see . . . Obviously it's improvised, but we have a rough storyboard so . . . um . . . five out of seven?

Doon

Okay, it's looking less like a goer. Will we be seeing this violence?

TV Exec
In what way?

Doon
Well, will it be implied, as in off screen, like all
great Greek drama? Or pornographised – as in
laid out in all its gory detail: rape, murder,
torture, chopping up and dead on a slab?

TV Exec
Oh, well, we would obviously have to see what
the story requires . . .

Slabs and more slabs. The stubbornness and
lack of creativity was exhausting. This was a new,
innovative, dynamic, never-done-before, female-led,
sassy cop show . . . yet it was the same old story.

Before I even got to read or improvise, I made
my excuses and left. How deflating that there was
nothing new in this 'original' new show, just the
familiar, predictable tropes. Surely we can tell some
other stories. As Rebecca Solnit says, ' What other
stories can be told? How do people recognise that
they have the power to be storytellers, not just
listeners?'

Viewers have great power too. Enjoying a rape

191

scene with your Merlot and cheese straw? Then you are part of what is feeding the beast. You *are* the ratings that make them push a bit further next time. All the streaming platforms, with more and more content needed. Please can we change the mindless consumption? The overeating and gorging on violence, which is (literally) killing us?

Nineteen

The Complicit PA

Casting Call

Sondra is mid-fifties, impeccably turned out and the PA to an immensely powerful film executive. She is efficient, no-nonsense and knows how to handle a 'difficult man' whose mercurial rages are the stuff of legend. She has weathered the storms and been his most long-standing employee when most have been fired. She thrives on the buzz, the private jets, the sudden trips to China for a casting, the money, the adrenaline. She has turned a blind eye to his indiscretions.

The summer before the pandemic hit, I landed an audition with David Mamet for his new play *Bitter Wheat*, starring John Malkovich. I was willing the play to be good, for me to have a decent part. It's Mamet. It's Malkovich. Please, God.

It was based on Weinstein. My part was the complicit PA, who had allowed many actresses to be abused and had turned a blind eye. A fascinating character, but sadly underwritten – only by a whisker, though. It was enough – yes, I would do the audition. What a privilege to work with Malkovich. Mamet was to direct and would be in the audition. I had studied Mamet at Manchester Uni and been mildly aware of the controversy surrounding his play *Oleanna*. Consequently, I read his plays and essays in preparation, although I didn't delve too much into his politics. I had read Rose McGowan's memoir, *Brave*, about her dealings with Weinstein and had had lunch twice with one of his PAs. In short, I prepared. I didn't feel well in the audition. In fact, I had a temperature of a hundred. My agent texted me a 'strong arm' emoji.

As soon as I entered the room, Mamet and I started sparring. I thought, I can handle this. I can make him laugh. He seems to respect strong women. I'm not afraid of him.

His opening gambit was: 'So, it says ventriloquism on your CV. Can you do some?'

I still don't know if that was real or a joke. I had told him I had just done my Ancestry DNA and found out that I had Spanish, Romanian, Celtic and Jewish genes. We joked about me being a Flamenco Jew. Spirits were high, like my temperature. I got the job.

I spent two weeks learning the script, then on the first day of rehearsals I took the 77 bus to Jerwood rehearsal space in Waterloo. I walked in. Mamet, effusive, built like a bulldog, compact, effervescent and focused, introduced me to John Malkovich. He was charming, laid-back, almost zen-like, wearing incredibly cool clothes. He shook my hand and said, 'Shall we run?'

I wasn't a hundred per cent sure what he meant. I was super-nervous and wondered, 'Shall we go for a run? Shall we run out of the room screaming?' But he obviously meant lines. So, we dispensed with the normal chit-chat, tea and coffee, introductions, meet-and-greet, read-through palaver and started running lines. The first week was just the two of us. What a joy.

John was an instinctive theatre animal, very easy, calming to Mamet's explosive energy. Efficiently, we would follow Mamet's mercurial instructions and then run lines without blocking and Mamet would say, 'Well, I'm a fucking idiot! Forget everything I just said and do what you did just then.'

He liked the words to do the job, not the actor.

'Don't describe anything. I don't want to see how hard you're working, what you had for fucking breakfast.'

No pauses allowed. No frills. Bam! Bam! Bam!

The entire cast was required to be present at all the rehearsals, like he needed, even fed on, our approval.

When I was in rather noisy shoes to practise walking in heels, he threw his hands up in exasperation, his deep Chicago/New York docker's accent full of sarcasm.

'Doon's making a lot of noise. Bang! Bang! Bang! Down goes the iPad. Bang! Bang! Bang! Down goes the phone. Clip-clop. Clip-clop.' All the while doing an impression of me, like a bull in a china shop.

I refused to take it. Cue my Marilyn Monroe accent: fluffy, vulnerable, American.

'Oh, I'm sorry, Mr Mamet. I forgot I'm a woman. I need to shush and be quiet and just tiptoe over here so no one can see me. Anyway, here's your coffee. Shh!'

A deathly silent pause, before Mamet declared: 'Well, that's me told!'

He looked to the other actors for support. No one flinched.

I was quick to retort. 'Yes, that is you told.' (Subtext: 'Don't you fucking tell me to be quiet.')

I felt exhilarated, but it was never easy to stand up to him. Any time one of the younger actors suggested any comedy business or invention, he was immediately shut down by Mamet in a withering and often offensive way. He sadly stopped making suggestions and instead just had to toe the line and do as directed.

On the first day, a stage manager was fired – perhaps he didn't like her tone. As I say, it was never easy.

Week three (we only have three weeks' rehearsal), and Mamet was in something of a panic to nail down exactly what the tone of the play is. I felt deeply uneasy. I didn't sign up for a farce about rape – I wanted this to really pack a punch and shine a light on all of Weinstein's evil. I'd been asked by the theatre owner to write something in the pro- gramme about what drew me to the play, in the light of the already negative feedback we'd had from some women saying 'hands off our story'. There was already a Twitter storm before the show had opened, yet again about a man writing about misogyny, outraged that women have, again, been left unable to tell their story. Mamet wrote a piece for the programme about the play being a farce. Again, I felt deeply uneasy about this and told the theatre manager I didn't want it included. She agreed. I did a Q&A with Ioanna Kimbrook, who played the abused girl, about why we stood by the play. Weinstein and his story triggered the #MeToo movement which, I feel, has begun to safeguard woman across the professions. When he was put in prison in real life, it felt like an enormous watershed moment. A profoundly uncomfortable scene in the play where he moves in on his victim in a hotel room as she escapes by ringing a fire alarm is a hugely important one. There are many other stories to be told. Many of the reviewers found my part underwritten. I was encouraged by the desire to look more deeply at the extent to which women were complicit in male abuse, but this wasn't that play.

Expectations are very high when Mamet puts pen to paper. Critics were very quick to do their job, but here was a man writing about a bully, centring the male perspective and looking at the astonishing delusion of an egomaniac with money who thought he had conquered the world and could do anything he liked and get away with it. I wrote at the time: 'His trial has just started. I won't hold my breath. These men are still in power and we are still pawns with small voices. We're getting louder.'

The wages I had been offered were under half what I'd got ten years ago in *Boeing-Boeing*, and it was a virtual three-hander. I came out of that show in debt, due to the fact that I was renting in London, but I gained several great new friends, had been seen by a lot of casting agents and had been very well reviewed. I didn't regret it for one minute.

At the end of the run I wrote Mamet a letter. It was just to let him know that we're doing a play about sexual exploitation and the gender pay gap and your lead actress can't pay her rent. Just in case you didn't know. He wrote me back, praising my genius as an actress but adding, 'Regarding your dilemma, as the ancient Greeks would say, sometimes the dog wins, sometimes the rabbit wins.'

Twenty

The Disruptor

Casting Call

Late-fifties mother of three, still angry, still fighting the patriarchy, still paying the bills, walking the dog and managing a career. She doesn't get her shopping delivered, is afraid of technology and prefers spray cans to tweets. Needs to see the other side of 'the story'. Can be 'inflexible'.

On the last day of *Bitter Wheat* – a Saturday in May – I find myself at 6 a.m. in Waterloo, clutching a can of pink Day-Glo spray paint. I assumed the street at that time would be deserted, but not so. A large Warburton's van unloads bread into a newsagent's, a surprising amount of people pepper the pavement. And my target, a cutting-edge London theatre, had someone arranging tables and chairs outside. At 6 a.m.? This is madness. In my head, the scene was empty. I would run in, do the deed and get the hell out. The spray can rattled in my bag. I sat down on a bench about twenty yards from the theatre and waited for a lull. My resolve was waning. Just go home, I lectured myself. There's cameras everywhere and you don't want to wear a mask. What are you thinking? Do you want everyone to know it's you?

But I knew I would do it. Adrenaline was shooting through my body, the spray can had the heaviness of a small gun, and it, too, could get me arrested. I walked to and fro in front of the theatre surveying the territory. There were still too many people about, but the man in 'front of house', as we call it in the business, had mercifully disappeared. I needed to do it.

Do it, Doon.

Do it.

Just do it.

A small, smouldering nugget, an ember of rage caught a tiny flame. I reached into my bag and pulled out the can. The militancy of the Eighties surged into my subconscious: scaling ladders up to huge billboards at 2 a.m., spraying huge cocks next to car exhausts; dangerous, exhilarating defacements of sexist ads – and here I was nearly forty years later, still angry and wanting to make my voice heard, to protest. There were six posters in a line outside the theatre advertising the current show. Yes, there was a camera looking straight at me. Yes, I lifted the can up to the first poster for the first letter. S. The nozzle seemed to be jammed. It fizzed and spurted, dripping down my hand. I shook it, my heart hammering. Suddenly, it jetted out, and I drew a large, wobbly S in delightfully bright pink neon paint. On the first poster, and then on until I had written STOLEN across the row of six posters.

It feels good – a renegade fifty-seven-year-old holding a spray can, graffitiing one of my favourite theatres in London. I don't dare look round. The traffic is building up. I feel I'm nearly there. E. I look up, straight into a camera, knowing it's likely I will never work here again. I feel a pang of sadness – I love this theatre, but I hate and detest what they've done to two women writers. Finally, N. Now time to survey the work. I am calm. I pop the can back into my bag, heart pounding, and head for the car. I feel elated. A small triumph in the big scheme of things, but one woman's protest nonetheless.

As I drive by I take a photo. It looks surprisingly good – STOLEN blazes out in neon pink across the posters. It says absolutely everything it needs to say.

I first heard about this story from a dear friend, a long and complicated story that is as old as time. Two women are brought in by a well-known star to turn his album into a possible musical. They have a contract. They work closely with him for four years, developing a script, honing it in workshops. But when the theatre gets hold of it and offers them the possibility of a run there with the final piece, everything changes. In effect, the women are dropped from the project, silenced and threatened with legal action if they speak up. More bullying.

It's shocking and woeful. I spoke to both of these women. They could not believe it had happened. They were afraid. They were suddenly redundant. As the director of the workshops said, if you rework the Bible, you still say 'created by God'. The poster only bore the men's names. The show was a hit, and they had got away with it. I needed to make a protest in however small a way. Yet another story of women silenced and blocked at one of our theatres. The tale as old as time.

Twenty-One

The Sexy Older Woman

Casting Call
Um . . . sorry . . . we gave the part
to a twenty-five-year-old.

What are the roles for older women? They tend to be few and far between. I rejoice when I see the brilliant Frances McDormand on screen as she is one of the few older actresses who hasn't had 'work'. We are simply not allowed to look our age as women. Many actresses who have work could be twenty or sixty, and begin to lose their unique beauty, instead morphing into an augmented version of 'perfection'. Most actresses succumb to the needle, knife or fillers simply to keep working (as one actress said to me, 'have work to keep working'). Everybody seems to be having Botox, and it's hard to look in the mirror without cringing.

We rarely see a heroine or love interest as an older woman, but there is a veritable feast of craggy older men being heroic. Here are five women's stories from history I would like to see played by the forgotten ranks of our feisty older actresses:

1) Born in 1740, French botanist Jeanne Baret was the first female to circumnavigate the globe. Had to dress as a man, obviously. Had no education. Many of her discoveries were attributed to the male botanist she travelled with, Philibert Commerson.

2) Born in 1931, Barbara Hillary was the first Black woman to reach the North Pole (at the age of seventy-five) and the South Pole (aged seventy-nine).

3) Born in 1775, Madame Ching (Zheng Yi Sao) was the most successful pirate of all time and ruled the Chinese seas. At one point, she commanded over four hundred pirate ships and sixty thousand pirates. She later ran a gambling house.

4) Born c. 442 BC, the Spartan princess Kyniska was the first female charioteer and the first woman

to win at the Olympic Games. She won with a team of horses she had trained herself. Her achievement had a great impact on women across the Greek world.

5) Born in 1848, Belle Star was a bandit queen, American outlaw, horse stealer, famous for wearing black velvet plumed hats. Shot in 1889 in mysterious circumstances.

In her fascinating *Almanac*, Sandy Toksvig lists literally hundreds of choices, from Brazilian bandit queens to Pussy Riot. Why aren't we watching them on screen?

And, for that matter, it's worth interrogating what is considered 'old' in our culture? Is it forty, fifty, sixty? Sixty-five-plus? What is acceptable sexually for an older woman? To accept a peaceful decline of libido, to settle into compatibility with your long-term partner, or to head back out there if you happen to be single? To internet date on Toyboy Warehouse? Or, if that makes you feel queasy, then perhaps Go-Go Grandad? Must we waste away? The clusterfuck of menopause, brain fog and bits of the body just going a bit wrong. Atrophy is the word that seems to be bandied about.

Our wombs are not the easiest of organs to

manage, especially after three children and a lung disease causing a persistent cough. So I sought some expertise regarding this, and went to King's College to see a gynaecologist. There was a waiting room of uncomfortable women of all ethnicities and a consultant of the very worst sort, frowning and bustling around impatiently in his high-waisted trousers and pressed pink shirt, mispronouncing any non-Caucasian names.

His manner is brusque, entitled. His brow is furrowed, his voice public school. I pray this is not my man. But, eventually, he locks eyes and announces my name. I sweep past him, refusing to shuffle or creep like the other ladies. He hates me already. A grim scene awaits. The chair. Two nurses are present (the sight of whom makes me sigh in relief). They instruct me to remove clothes below the waist and, indeed, 'pop your feet into the stirrups'. The legs are wide. I have a useless medical gown draped over my lap. Everybody chats. And he's here, Pink Shirt, snapping on the latex gloves like Gillian Anderson in *The Fall*. He has a brusque jolliness about him. He has seen it all before. He has stared into a thousand vulvas, and there is a hint of deviance or misogyny about him. One or the other or both. The lubricant is scooped rather too slowly onto the gloved fingers.

The Sexy Older Woman

I sit back with a nonchalant rictus expression embedded into my jaw and he's in – quick, deft twist of the wrist, up, up and away. He is owning the area. Swivel. And all the time he is looking rather too deeply into my eyes. And then it comes.

Pink Shirt
Don't I know you from somewhere?

A sort of electrical tingle of shame and anger shoots up my spine. I'm speechless. Should I be nice, affable, grateful? Fuck no! Pause. Breathe.

Doon
(*slow but dark*)
Now is not the time.

He glances to the other nurses for support. They look awkward. He is the alpha male.

Pink Shirt
(*an amused smile playing on his lips*)
Yes, but I *do* know you from somewhere. Don't I?

It's a sort of *Carry On* scenario, but I'm not Barbara Windsor, giggling. I'm now a tornado of

Greek heroines (Clytemnestra, Medea). He is treating me as a puppet at the end of his arm.

Doon
Now is not the time.

His patronising smile dies instantly and morphs to one of pure disdain. He removes his arm brusquely, snaps off his gloves while raising his eyes to the nurses at the flagrant telling-off he has had. I will place bets that has never happened before. I still sit legs apart. He goes to a small table, grabs a pen and paper, and starts a little drawing. I'm thinking, perhaps a sorry note?

The nurses look to him, but he is busy scribbling. Finally, a curt nod. Then he shows me a crude biro drawing of my womb and cervix. He is clearly furious and wants me out.

Pink Shirt
So, there is bulging here at the vaginal walls, a prolapse (*he indicates his rough sketch of womb bulging*). The womb is pushing through, so we will put a mesh here to bind it, and while we're up there we will enter here and whip the womb out at the same time. (*Brandishes a*

crude biro sketch to show where the womb
will be evacuated.)

Doon
My womb? Why do you have to take my
womb out?

Pink Shirt
(*snorting*)
Well, you don't really need it any more, do you?

I like my womb. If it's not absolutely essential that it comes out, could you leave it there, please? It's been the garden for three babies. It's held and cradled and rocked them in its salty, watery gloom. To think that it could have been needlessly removed thanks to the medical misogyny so patently on display is astonishing. This doctor was furious at my answering back and asking him to please get on with his job rather than discussing my CV at such a compromising moment, so in retaliation he would take a precious piece of me out, potentially causing untold, long-term problems. I decided to complain about Pink Shirt. He got 'a warning', whatever that is. I got a second opinion and was prescribed some physiotherapy which sorted everything out. So, please, do always get a second opinion, and never trust a man in a pink shirt.

The next TV role I took (I wonder if Pink Shirt was watching?) was pretty much 'sexy older woman'. I was fifty-seven, and was to play the lead's boss: twice his age, feisty, good at her job, single. Normally, the trappings of this sort of role – an 'up for it', game old bird who'd shag anything – also include a sort of desperate last-hurrah fruitiness. A sexually frustrated businesswoman, whose career has overtaken her and left her childless but horny. We could rewind to 'The Desperate Cougar'. Young man! Be afraid! Here she comes, the big spider! She's going to catch you in her middle-aged web and eat you alive. The lone she-wolf, prowling at the edges of parties, stalking for young meat. I often sense this, if meeting a group of men at a party, pub, gathering, that because I am single I am somehow 'up for it'. An awful sort of laddish banter springs up – I'm a threat to their relationships. I'm obviously looking for sex and often the conversation gets 'worryingly sexual'. I find it thoroughly depressing.

So often, if any sex is involved, casting calls for older women make her out as a nymphomaniac, a lonely nutter or a threat to someone's safe marriage.

A sort of 'bet she would throw you round the bedroom', nudge-nudge, unspoken camaraderie between the men. So, it was with great relief that I accepted the role of the older woman in a Channel 4 series called *Pure* about a young woman with pure OCD, based on a true story which had been turned into a memoir. This is the sexual type of OCD, where every encounter is seen by the sufferer in a sexual way. It treated this very real affliction with humour and honesty, and I loved the scripts. There was a lot of nudity and sex in her thoughts and projections that we saw on screen, but it was handled in a non-voyeuristic, highly sensitive way. It felt totally non-gratuitous. If we saw breasts, we also saw penises, male buttocks, everything. It's a fine line, but the tone and the way it's shot is everything.

The protagonist's friend (my love interest) had an addiction to porn, which he was coming to the end of treatment for, and he wanted his job back with me. There was some flirty banter after his welcome-back dinner, a taxi ride where we kissed, and then after a few days we had sex. The big difference in this role was that my character was anything but a desperate cougar. If anything, he did the chasing. He pursued. She was unsure. She finally invites him over, and they have sex, but on his terms due to his past addictions. He finds it hard to have 'normal' heterosexual sex unless he is doing things to her but he also suffers from erectile dysfunction. She realises that perhaps he isn't the right person 'to heal with', so she tries to finish it. He begs her not to, even offers to use Viagra, but she ends it. A woman turning down a beautiful man half her age because it's not really working for her. This is radical. We never see this. There is nothing desperate or predatory about her.

I found that role liberating. Unsurprisingly, it was written, adapted, produced and directed by women. It may seem minor, but storylines like that, which challenge the dreadful stereotypes of older women, we need to see a lot more of. There are so many older actresses we never see, because the parts aren't there or we are resigned to being typecast as mad, on the scrap heap, cat-obsessed. This is what we are used to. There are many stories about older men, craggy, complicated, paunchy, often with their very young wives, girlfriends or mistresses. I hope you're all right with nudity, ladies – if you want this part you'll probably have to get naked.

Speaking of nudity, when shooting *Toast of London* I was unaware – or rather 'not informed' – of a lingering shot of a naked woman on stage in one episode that was utterly gratuitous. I complained to the writer and said it needed to be balanced by seeing a penis. An eye for an eye, so to speak. So, in one storyline I get to hang out as Toast's agent at a gay pool party. A naked gay pool party. But there was not a penis in sight. Buttocks? Yes. The reason? Too expensive. Cocks cost a lot more on screen than lady parts. Of course they do, silly me.

The next role I took was for a Netflix series, *The Duchess* – radical in that I was the hated ex-husband's new fiancée but – the big twist – I was actually a 'really nice woman'. Kind, helpful, funny. This is incredibly rare. (The 'other woman' usually bitches, backstabs, stirs things up, refuses access to children, and is jealous and insecure – again, a whole string of stereotypes.) Plus I was twice the ex-husband's age but not a cougar, not ridiculous, just sassy, funny and rather sweet. It was probably because it was written by Katherine Ryan, a smart, sexy, funny and kind woman herself. Although there was no second series, it was interesting the number of young fem-inists I spoke to who loved my character, because they said they had rarely, or never, seen a genuinely 'nice woman' on screen who wasn't a put-upon mum or 'mouse'. 'Nice' is rare. It was a very empowering and enjoyable role.

Sassy, mature, feisty, not perfect, funny, complicated, real, messy heroines – where are they? I am sure their stories are being pitched; they are just not commissioned. Or they take second fiddle to their 'hero'. We just can't quite let go of the male hero, the adventurer, the saviour, the damaged one. With his handmaids all around him. We must put women back in the centre of the story, and it goes without saying, in writing, commissioning, producing and directing too. When can we step off this treadmill into new, fresher pastures? Even the men who purport to agree with these sentiments do not want to relinquish their power. They have calcified in their caves and refuse to come out. We are far from equal and we are tired of just chipping away, inching forward with small victories. It's time to get the explosives out.

Twenty-Two

The Hag

Casting Call
Grotesque, half-woman/half-beast, malevolent witch, warty face and hairy hands, with a cackle to send ice down the spine. She is mercifully, brutally murdered at the climax of the film by our hero, to the villagers' joy, but they all still use the medicines she prescribed as a younger witch. Five-chinned, detestable and repulsive, can hardly be called a 'woman'.

I had been asked several times to do panto. In my mind, it's a bit like my frequently being asked to do *I'm a Celebrity . . . Get Me Out of Here!* Every year, the money improved for both projects, but neither interested me. I love children's joy at the pantomime, and I occasionally like watching it. But the jungle is truly ghastly. I was offered so much money one year I actually took the meeting. Quite a few of my friends like the show. My brother and sister-in-law watch it religiously. People seem desperate to see me in it. Oh, go on, Doon! You'll win it! You'll be hilarious! I can just see the front page of *The Sun*, me glaring furiously mid-feminist-rant at some Jim Davidson type over the campfire. Hilarious!

I can't quite believe I did go to the meeting. The two producers were very affable, very chatty. 'It's just a comedy, really.'

I disagree. In my opinion, it's a voyeuristic, painful psychological experiment that is damaging to animals and humans alike, a dumbing-down of TV, a crass melting pot of 'strange celebrities', ex-singers, presenters, actors.

As these cheery producers tucked into their blackened cod at a posh West End restaurant, allaying my fears between mouthfuls, fluffing up the show, I suddenly felt actually and overwhelmingly sick. I did a very bad piece of acting, where I pretended I had a voice-over I had forgotten about, and practically ran out of the restaurant while they were still eating. The money I could have got would have allowed me to be mortgage-free and more. We are all, of course, on a sliding scale of hypocrisy versus politics, so I didn't do 'The Jungle' but I did do panto.

It was a lot of money, and I would miss a family Christmas, but that had to be sacrificed. I was to play the Wicked Queen in a huge theatre where, from the back row, the stage was the size of a mobile phone screen. Vast stacks of speakers, so much better suited to a rock concert. On stage you couldn't hear laughter, only the screams! There was a cavernous space between the musicians and the front row: in short, zero atmosphere. In two weeks, I had to learn six dance routines and two solo songs. There were twenty-five twenty-five-year-olds, and I was the grand dame. I had never danced or sung in a show before. I was wearing a knee brace, as I'd injured myself trying to get fit on a paddle board in Hastings the week before, and with my dodgy lungs the dances were exhausting. But it was a fun challenge. The acting was not so much fun. The director, a skinny blond Dracula, over-smiling, allowed no invention or deviation.

'Don't add a single line!' he would instruct, and then proceed to read all my lines in a ghastly drawl replete with ghastly panto laugh. 'Darling, less is more. All the greats know that.'

Like a terrible, frustrated turn, he would do my walk, my laugh, and steal every ounce of invention or joy from what should have been a bit of a laugh. It was the first time I felt I had done a job purely for the money, and I absolutely hated it. I was actually working out how much I earned per hour, I was so miserable.

I flagged up some ghastly sexist lyrics and had to rewrite them. (Dracula was furious at this but smiled on through.) The lyrics were along the lines of: 'She's the Queen but she's old and minging' (to the tune of 'You're just too good to be true'). Sung to me by the Prince. 'You're just too old to be true, I think I'm going to spew.'

Do you hear that, kiddies? Old women are 'disgusting', ragged old brasses, and eww!, some of them still flirt. It takes 'desperate cougar' to a whole new level – the old Queen coming on to the Prince who is physically sickened by her appearance and her 'smell'. So, I could change some of the lyrics but not the overall stereotypes.

The wicked Queen's dress, heavy with the sweat of a thousand Anita Dobsons, was a vast velvet gown that couldn't be washed. Instead, it was just sprayed with vodka around the armpit area after each show. The train of the dress (think Princess Diana, but in red velvet) had to be held by an elastic wristband that cut off the blood supply, and as my arms were aloft for most of the show – incanting, bringing in the magic mirror from the gods, cursing, dancing, twerking – my batwings vanished, but so did my will to live. My dressing room was a windowless bunker next to the stage that vibrated to the 250,000kw speakers just outside. A couple of fruit flies patrolled my prison cell, even though there was no fruit in sight, nowhere to sit and put make-up on, and strip-lights to make you feel your most confident.

I lay on the floor to rest between the two shows a day and couldn't seem to eat much. After a week of breathing in the 'haze' smoke effects, my chest was causing me problems. I started to panic that I would get ill. Memories of pneumonia were never far from my mind. The dance routines were a struggle, as well as the songs. I would fall asleep between shows, full eye make-up on, and wake up with glitter in my eyeballs. I began to wake up feeling sick in my Airbnb in the mornings: exhaustion, dry eyes, general unhappiness. Towards the end of the run I had to have three shows off as I caught noro-virus. There was no understudy, so my guilt was enormous as one of the dancers had to go on with line prompts and my sweaty dress. I sent her a huge bunch of flowers, but I don't think it made up for the hell of those three shows for her. I managed the final four shows with sick buckets on either side of the wings, swallowing sick-burps as I navigated my way through the hideous and exhausting song-and-dance routines.

New Year's Eve was the last night. I came off stage, burst into tears and took the hated dress off, but was too exhausted to get dressed. I lay on the floor crying glitter tears. I went home without saying goodbyes. I went to bed at 10 p.m. and woke at midnight to the sound of a thousand fireworks heralding in the New Year and puked what seemed to be pure acid. The dancers, the singers, the other actors were all lovely. It was just not my tribe, and I had done it for the wrong reasons. But it did allow me to live during lockdown. I've turned down very many lucrative jobs because they involved 'selling out' in my eyes, or a direct clash with my politics. Adverts and voice-overs for pharmaceutical companies, McDonald's, De Beers diamonds to name a few . . . I'm not crowing – we all have to eat – but there is a line. I did panto purely for cash, and I was miserable.

The Hag

So, sexy older woman segues quickly into the Hag. Some recent castings offered to me were:

1) Non-speaking ogre
2) Very old maid

Curvature of the spine, palsied, hands shaking uncontrollably – is this now what I can look forward to? Do I need to get work done to keep working?

Katherine Ryan, creator and star of *The Duchess* has had a lot of work done to her face. She is very honest about this. But acting alongside her on screen, because her face resembles a creaseless pillow with bee-stung lips and pumped-up cheeks, I resemble 'a witch', full of wrinkles, a 'character' face. But because she doesn't look her age, I, with no work done, look so much older. It was painful for me to watch it. A perfect, flawless, totally line-free face next to a craggy, slightly ragged-looking older woman. This is one of the reasons it is so hard not to get work done, because a lot of actresses around you have. Whether you like what they look like, or think they look weird or not like themselves, they are still a sort of blank canvas rather than an Ordnance Survey map, the thread veins being all the little rivers along the way.

I had been told by shameless make-up ladies, who should be praising my lack of Botox or fillers or lifts, that they knew a very discreet place for 'a freshening' or 'a plumping'. But I have resisted. Sometimes it is hard. Sometimes, after seeing myself in particularly gruelling high-definition, I take myself to the mirror and take a long hard look and try to congratulate myself. Yes, I'm ageing. But I look like myself. I'm expressive. I'm fifty-nine, and I'm an actor who is weathering the storm and working without cutting or needles or fillers. Am I brave, or stupid? How long is my shelf life? Is it all ogres and hags? Will I just be the joke character, the cameo, the strict, the shouty, the bossy, the sex starved?

Our daughters are in a frightening pandemic of hating themselves, of getting surgery at eighteen, of cutting away their fat, of changing their faces, not to mention suffering from a whole host of mental health issues. There is too much pressure. Social media has stoked a dangerous fire and they are burning. The best lesson I can give to an anxious young girl is not to inject or cut my face, to say whatever society says, that I am beautiful as I am. My mother telling me I should have a nose job when I was sixteen has given me a hatred of my nose. I see it in profile in the cinema and think 'Run! Run for your life!' But I've worked on accepting myself. My brave, regal face. By tampering, I believe we are saying to our daughters that we are not good enough. We hate ourselves so we are going to self-harm with surgery. There is not another face like yours. Like the trillions and trillions of snowflakes, it is unique.

It is not so much the categorising of Botox into a 'treat package' that a recent *Guardian* beauty editor described and indulged in 'a couple of times a year'. Fresh versus stale. It is not what we do with needles or knives – we are fully entitled to do what we want to our faces – but it's the legacy to the younger generation. It's the disgust women and girls feel about ageing that is the issue, the deep anxiety pervading girls and young women who already hate themselves. This is a very dangerous game, and we must be mentors. If I continue to age on stage and screen with grace and dignity, accepting my face and the way it is changing, remaining confident, sassy, mischievous, then I am sending a powerful message to counter the malaise that is pervasive among young women and girls. Women everywhere have begun to hate their faces and their bodies, and believe they need to be changed to survive in this very harmful culture. You can practically pop to your corner shop and get your face changed.

Aesthetic clinics are everywhere with shaming pictures of sagging jowls and cellulite buttocks – only women's, of course. I delight in taking my Sharpie pen with me everywhere and defacing these clinics with the message, 'No thanks, I'm beautiful as I am.' If only women could get back to believing that.

Epilogue

The Crow

I'm sixty. It's New Years' Day, 2023, dawn, around 5.45 a.m. I'm walking down Bottle Alley, a covered half-mile promenade where countless pieces of multicoloured glass bottles are embedded in the concrete. The sea is a tumultuous great swell to my right – I can feel the spray on my face. I'm dressed as a crow in a vast, feathered black coat, the head and beak pushed back off my face. Earlier in the evening, I had been out to see a drag show around nine, getting home at two thirty. Then I went out again to seek my kids at a club on the seafront. Going out again? At half two in the morning? Aged sixty? Two times a lady? Not on any drugs? But, it must be said, a few shots of tequila.

Now, clip-clopping home alone in my heels down the long, long seafront to my house in the old town. And I feel good. Excited about the year ahead. I made it. From Wild Child to The Crow, I made it – still dancing, still laughing, still loving, still working, still swimming and still fighting. And there is still a lot to fight for. To be seen, to be included in the stories that our culture is telling. To be respected at all ages. To feel safe in this dangerous, ugly climate. To stop hating ourselves and our bodies. To be proud of our strong beliefs, not shamed, diminished, silenced. To create stories that nourish and inspire, not scar or deflate. To go out blazing in your crow coat, dancing to drum and bass. Bold, free and fearless. And so . . .

What will you do now?

Acknowledgements

Huge thanks to Marcella Sutcliffe for the week at Chapel Garth which kicked it all off. To the essential typists (as I write longhand): Lucy Scott, the queen who typed 90,000 words from a Dictaphone, all hail! To Aunty Christine for endless days of dictation in Hastings and your humour and patience. To India, for many long days of dictation during revisions and her inspiring support. To my mother Barbara, the source, the original 'rebel' and rule-breaker for her memories and unique character and of course for giving me 'FRED', the African grey free-flying parrot who can squarely be blamed for my acting career. To Rocky, dearly departed Dad who inspired us all with his comedy, characters, songs and wonderful jokes, his kindness and curiosity.

To my book group of 25 years, Anne, Judy, Robin, Jacquie, Sarah, Jenny and Lucy for endless support and discussions and rallying. Thank you,

Jenny Landreth, for direction and wise-words, Brenda Gilhooly for fanning the flames, Martha Hammick for support and excellent 'chats', Arabella Weir for fine stories from the frontline, April de Angelis for reigniting old memories and strong support. To my brother Blair and partner Anna for providing a retreat, a safe-haven, a hospital during illness, dog-sitting service and sustenance, laughter and kitchen-dancing. To sister Sheena, to Sharon (my angel), to Norval for the four house-moves during the writing of the book, to the amazing WOW swimmers (without wetsuits) for the everyday essential medicine swims at 9 a.m., fisherman's beach, to Sandi Toksvig for expert advice, to Stella the Staffy for invaluable walks and love, to universal credit for barely letting us live during the pandemic.

Thanks to my agent Jo Unwin for sticking with me and rallying when I abandoned it and lost hope, to Helena Gonda, editor extraordinaire, for expert cutting, shaping and midwifery, not to mention days of typing. To Hannah Knowles for steering me early on, and finally to Canongate for faith and the commission, I am so happy to be under this radical bird's wing. To my most excellent agents at Hamilton Hodell and finally to my children, India, Louis and Ella for helping me make sense of it all. I hope the

Acknowledgements

book helps you make sense of me. You have truly given me the greatest happiness.

To Loch Tay, the English Channel, Brockwell and Tooting Lido, the River Brede, the Hebridean Sea and the Atlantic. The water helped the words.

Further Reading and Select Bibliography

Non-fiction and memoir

Andrea Dworkin, *Pornography: Men Possessing Women*

Audre Lorde, *When I Dare to be Powerful: Women so empowered are dangerous*

Buchi Emecheta, *Second-Class Citizen*

Christiane Ritter, *A Woman in the Polar Night*

Clarissa Pinkola Estes, *Women Who Run With the Wolves: Myths and Stories of the Wild Woman Archetype*

Dale Spender, *Man Made Language*

Emma Goldman, *Living My Life*

Fay Weldon, *Auto Da Fay*

Georgia Pritchett, *My Mess Is a Bit of a Life: Adventures in Anxiety*

Gloria Steinem, *My Life on the Road*

Jill Posener, *Spray It Loud*

Kat Banyard, *The Equality Illusion: Truth about Women and Men Today*

Mary Wollstonecraft, *A Vindication of the Rights of Woman*

Mary Ann Sieghart, *The Authority Gap: Why women are still taken less seriously than men, and what we can do about it*

Meilssa Febos, *Body Work: The Radical Power of Personal Narrative*; *Girlhood*

Nan Shepherd, *The Living Mountain*

Natasha Walter, *Living Dolls: The Return of Sexism*

Phyllis Chesler, *Women and Madness*

Sandi Toksvig, *Almanac*

Sandra Gilbert and Susan Gubar, *The Madwoman in the Attic: The Woman Writer and the Nineteenth-Century Literary Imagination*

Sheila Rowbotham, *Hidden From History*

Simone de Beauvoir, *The Second Sex*

Sonya Renee Taylor, *The Body is Not An Apology: The Power of Radical Self-love*

Novels and Plays

Anaïs Nin, *The Veiled Woman*

Fay Weldon, *Mischief*

Federico García Lorca, *The House of Bernarda Alba and other Plays*

Jean Rhys, *Wide Sargasso Sea*

Toni Morrison, *Beloved*